H. C. Taylor

CREATIVE RELATIONSHIP

*Science and Religion
in the Twenty-First Century*

CREATIVE RELATIONSHIP

*Science and Religion
in the Twenty-First Century*

Herbert C. Taylor,
B.Ph., B.D., M. Div.

Rutledge Books, Inc. Danbury, CT

Rutledge Books, Inc.
107 Mill Plain Road, Danbury, CT 06811
1-800-278-8533
www.rutledgebooks.com

Manufactured in the United States of America

Cataloging in Publication Data
Taylor, Rev. Herbert C.
   Creative Relationship: Science and Religion in the
      Twenty-First Century.

   ISBN: 1-58244-108-1

   1. Science. 2. Religion. 3. Relationship with God.

Library of Congress Card Number: 00-112199

This book is dedicated to:

Dr. Kenneth L. Wilson
President Emeritus of the Board of Directors,
a friend and fellow resident in the Retirement Community
where I live, who read the manuscript as it was in process
of being written, and urged me to get it published.

TABLE OF CONTENTS

PREFACE

Religion and Science have been in a competitive relationship, for the most part, throughout the second millenium. At the beginning of that period and for the most of human history, religion as an explanation and guide in human affairs has been dominant. Science, in the sense of organized knowledge, has been current throughout human history, but it has never had the dominance that it has received in the twentieth century. Humans, however, have always had the mental capacity to formulate their knowledge of the world around them into ideas that will help them to cope with its challenges to some degree. Their religion, too, has developed to help them deal with the uncertainties and mysteries that they did not understand. Since most of what happened in their world was beyond their understanding, religion played a dominant role in their thinking.

Around the middle of the second millenium this situation started to change. It had already begun to change some centuries earlier in the Muslim countries, which were free from the dominance of the Roman Catholic Church that exercised almost complete control over the centers of learning in Europe. However, with the Reformation which began around 1500 AD, the power of the Church of Rome was challenged in both religious and scientific matters. Free Universities were established in the countries that had thrown off the Roman yoke, and even in those in largely Catholic countries breathed some of the air of free thought.

Budding scientists, such as Copernicus and Galileo,

advanced theories based on observations that contradicted the biblical world views and opened the eyes of many to the new concepts of astronomy: an earth that was a planet of the sun, similar to other heavenly bodies such as Venus, Mars, Jupiter, and Saturn. New optical instruments revealed wonders such as mountains on the moon and rings around Saturn. Gradually a new science of astronomy was born. Similar new concepts emerged in the study of planet earth, such as that of gravity and new ideas in human nature and origins, and in medicine.

Slowly, at first, and then with increasing rapidity as the 17th, 18th, and 19th Centuries came and went, a body of new scientific knowledge developed and grew. With the growth of science as an explanation of the world and the universe around us, the "unknown" shrunk in area, and the concept of the Supernatural declined with it both in meaning and in value. As the twentieth Century passed, many religious leaders recognized that the scientific understanding of the world around us has grown to such an extent that most religious concepts of God's place and function in it are severely challenged. Some of them reacted by denouncing "science" and the impious scientists. They fought a retreating battle against scientific explanation that had replaced religious ones. Others joined forces with the advances in human understanding, and modified or rejected the so-called "supernatural" explanations of Theology as "outmoded."

Therefore, despite the efforts of conservative clerics and their mentors to downplay the role of science in human affairs, and to gain a greater role for the biblical views in basic and higher education, the scientist's view of the universe and man's place in it is reaching more and more of the populace who enjoy the benefits of scientific advance. One of the Church historians who was instrumental in my own theological education, put the problem into these words: "We have to evangelize the inevitable." Only as religion finds a place for science and its views, and promotes scientific thinking, will it continue to have relevance to humanity and the future. This book, then, is my own effort to help to evangelize the inevitable, as one who has had both religious training and theological studies along with a grounding in the various sciences through my education as an engineer, together with a long continuing interest in following the advance of scientific discovery through my reading. It is an effort to express my personal faith in God and his care for human beings, along with the rest of his creation, in terms that are scientifically relevant. It is up to you, the reader, to determine how well I have succeeded, and it may be, in the future, to improve on my efforts.

CHAPTER ONE

WHAT DO WE KNOW AND HOW DO WE KNOW IT?

"The question is, 'What did he know,
and when (how) did he know it?'"

— Senator Baker's inquiry regarding Richard Nixon's knowledge of the Watergate break-in and cover-up during the president's impeachment hearings, July 1974.

You, inquisitive readers, who presumably have opened this book in pursuit of more knowledge, are already the possessors of a great storehouse of learning. For example, the letters on this page are made up of printed shapes or forms, which you recognize, and which are combined into certain sequences which you also recognize as words and sentences. These sequences of inky forms on paper mean something to you. That is, they connect to information already stored somewhere in your brain to give you understanding of what I, the author, am trying to say, and quite possibly to initiate thoughts in your mind that have never occurred to mine.

Long ago, no doubt, you learned to read these sequences of shapes and associate them with your own experiences in daily life. Some words, like "chair" or "table," bring to your mind a specific kind of shape or form that you see and touch every day. Other words, such as "read" or "say," suggest certain kinds of behavior or activity. Still others, such as "like" or "dislike," "love" or "hate," signify to you certain feelings or emotions you may have.

Much of the information in the storehouse of our memories has come to us through reading, an activity that is a relatively recent achievement in the human quest for knowledge. In ancient civilizations reading and writing were rather specialized human skills, not shared by the majority of individuals who lacked the opportunity to acquire them. Not until Coster, Guttenberg, Caxton, and others developed the art of printing in the sixteenth century in Europe was a wider dispensing of information made possible and learning or education given a dramatic boost.

It was from the Chinese, who had discovered it about seven centuries earlier, that Europeans learned the art of printing, which facilitated the making of many books and the techniques of making the paper on which those books were printed. The languages of the Western world, using a phonetic alphabet, were much more adaptable than Chinese to this innovation in communication. Thus, in the span of five decades, from 1450 to 1500, books in Europe increased from a few tens of thousands to over ten million! What an explosion of knowledge!

Older than the art of printing by many millennia, of course, were writing and the reading of what was written. Writing developed gradually from primitive drawings, which appear in caves in various parts of the world dating back, possibly, some thirty thousand years. Such pictures, apparently, communicated information dealing with the hunt and the animals that were hunted. Perhaps, in some cases, they recorded spells or prayers that were believed to contribute to a successful hunt. Primitive peoples of a later period also seem to have tallied days, animals, or other objects by scratching marks on bones, stones, or sticks.

The most important step in the development of writing from such drawings or markings came about when the pictures or symbols began to represent not just an object but a sound, which was its name. In other words writing was a more symbolic form of drawing in which the symbols came to have a phonetic meaning. By about 3000 B.C.E., such symbolic writing appeared in wedged-shaped impressions on clay tablets, dried and preserved in the cities of the Sumerians that were located in Mesopotamia, in the Tigris and Euphrates river valleys. About the same time, or shortly thereafter, writing appears to have developed in the Nile River valley, the land of Egypt, a thousand miles to the west. Here the pictographs, or hieroglyphs, were carved on stone monuments, painted on walls or pottery, or, later, drawn on a kind of paper made from the fibers of the papyrus plant that grew abundantly along the banks of the Nile. In another five centuries writing was again invented, apparently quite independently, in Elam (present-day Iran), and almost simultaneously in the Indus river valley (present-day Pakistan.)

Another five centuries later it was used to record the yet unknown language of the civilization on the island of Crete. Perhaps the Cretans, or Minoans, as they called themselves, learned the art of writing from the Egyptians with whom they traded, but their scripts, now labeled "Linear A" and "Linear B," were highly original.

On the mainland around 1500 B.C.E., in what is present-day Turkey, the Hittites had invented their own writing style, and thousands of miles to the east, so had the Chinese.

A few centuries later, on the other side of the world and among a people unknown to any of the above civilizations, another form of writing was invented by the Maya Indians to keep an elaborate set of astronomical and historical records.

The making of books or even shorter documents by such handwriting crafts was long and laborious. Yet this did not deter those who wanted to set down a collection of what they considered to be vital information for their contemporaries and their posterity. The famous library at Alexandria, Egypt, which stored many of the writings of the ancient world from 400 B.C.E. to 300 B.C.E., is believed to have had, at one time, about a half to three-quarters of a million volumes! One of the volumes it housed was the Septuagint; a translation into Greek of the Hebrew scriptures (Old Testament) made by a group of seventy or seventy-two scholars.

The Israelites had begun to write down their history and religious traditions around 1,000 B.C.E., and included in them this commentary on the literary efforts of mankind: "...of making many books there is no end; and much study is a weariness of the flesh."[1]

I wonder what the writer of that observation might have had to say about such modern phenomena as a university library, the Library of Congress, or even the bookstore section of a modern department store. Truly a great proportion of our human knowledge has been committed to books, and a large part of what we know, individually, has come from them. For example, they are the source of most of what you will find herein.

But long before writing was invented human beings had spoken languages, and the means of sharing information with one another on a more limited basis. When humans first learned to talk with one another, inventing a language to do so, is lost in the mists of antiquity. Biblical literalists might claim they were created with this ability, since the third chapter of Genesis portrays Adam and Eve as talking to one another, to God, and even to a serpent. Evolutionary doctrine, however, theorizes that human language developed from the sounds made by our pre-human forebears. Many animals have special sounds of warning, mating calls, and other vocal signals that they use. Some, such as dolphins and whales, may even have a language of their own, though this has not been certainly established. But all the races of human beings have languages, and even among otherwise primitive peoples, these may be quite complex.

We can only speculate on how such languages began. No doubt specific sounds or series of sounds came to represent various objects; named them, in other words. The same probably applied to individuals who came to have names, too. It is quite likely that the vocal sounds of early language were accompanied by meaningful gestures and the unconscious "body language" that we still use. It has been shown that other members of the primate family to which we belong, namely chimpanzees and gorillas, though incapable of forming vocal words due, apparently, to their palate and mouth structures and, perhaps, to under-developed brain centers for speech, are yet able to learn and, to a degree, communicate in a sign language such as that taught to the deaf.

Thus our human ancestors in the evolutionary system appear to have learned to communicate their thoughts with one another, and to share their knowledge. And still, in our growing up from infancy to childhood, we all learn to recognize and to make the meaningful sounds that become our language. Much of what we know is communicated to us, or by us, in this way. Humans, in the animal world, are the greatest communicators.

Now, as we have seen, writing (reading) and speaking (listening) make use of symbolism. Words, written or spoken, are symbolic of the things we observe, the feelings that we have, or the actions that we undertake in our daily lives. We relate the series of letters or sounds to the various concepts preserved in our memories and thus we understand them.

What we read, of course, enters our minds through our sense of sight. Speech, in turn, comes into our consciousness through our sense of hearing. A blind person, however, may learn to read Braille through the sense of touch, or may use the sense of hearing to listen to someone else read, as in recorded readings or "talking books." A deaf person may learn to understand the spoken word by "reading" lips, or by "talking" with someone who has learned sign language. So, if one sense is impaired or missing, another may be substituted to communicate between one mind and another.

In addition, of course, we also learn more directly by way of our senses through seeing or observing, or through hearing sounds other than human speech, through our senses of touch and taste, and even, to some extent, through our sense of smell. The latter is not as highly developed in humans as in some other animals or in insects, but it is sufficient to warn us of the danger of fire through the smell of smoke, for example, or to attract us to members of the opposite sex through the use of perfume, cologne, or after-shave lotion.

While reading is important to the acquisition of a body of knowledge, and much time in formal education is therefore devoted to it, science, as body of knowledge about our surroundings, depends to a high degree on direct observation for its content and accuracy. In astronomy, physics, chemistry, geology, biology, etc., observation and experimentation (a testing of theories through careful observation under controlled circumstances) are of primary importance. In sciences dealing with human beings, their behavior and motivation, either in the present or the past, less observation and experimentation are possible, and, therefore, theories are harder to substantiate or totally reject. This is true, for example, in anthropology, history, medicine, psychology, economics, philosophy and, perhaps especially, in theology, which some would not even label a science.

In observation and experimentation, other senses besides sight, of course, have their part to play, but a disproportionate share of our direct knowledge depends upon our sense of sight. The human eye is such an extraordinary organ in enabling us to discern and deal with the world around us that the theologian has often referred to it as evidence of a providential design. However, the evolutionist can trace the development of the eye from light sensitivity in single-celled creatures on up through various stages of light-sensitive cells to the complex anatomy of the eye not just once but several times in the evolution of the many forms of life in our world. Yes, the human eye, despite its remarkable adaptation to its function of bringing to our brains a full color, stereoscopic, moving picture of the world around us during our waking hours, is constructed out of basically the same kind of living cells as our skin and skeleton.

The eye, as has often been suggested, is similar to a camera, though a very miniaturized and sophisticated one. It has a shutter (the eyelid), a lens with a protective covering (the cornea), an adjustable diaphragm to regulate the amount of light admitted (the iris), an automatic focusing mechanism that adjusts to the distance of the picture it is taking (an elastic lens that changes in convexity by the pull of muscle fibers), a light sensitive film on which the image formed by the cornea and lens may fall (the retina), and an automatic cleaning and lubricating mechanism (tears).

We have two such remarkable cameras, the images from which are automatically combined into one by the mind to provide us a three-dimensional image. The eye cameras, furthermore, are more like television cameras than ordinary still cameras, which take isolated pictures of action frozen at certain instants of time, or even like movie cameras, which take a series of photographic stills that give the illusion of motion when run through a projector at matching speed. Like the television camera, the eye translates the image falling on the retina into electrical impulses which travel through the nerve network and are translated back into images we can "see" in the "computer circuits" of the brain.

The retina is much more complex than any photographic film, but, like such a film, it records what we see through the action of light in altering certain chemicals. Two kinds of sensing cells are found in the retina, called rods and cones which, in a sense, "taste" what we "see." Experiments have shown that it is the rods that are most sensitive to the chemical changes made by light on certain substances in the retina. The cones, on the other hand, detect the subtle differences caused by the different colors and pass this information on to the brain. There are three different light sensitive chemicals in the cells of the retina that are decomposed by red, green, and violet light. Their decomposition products are detected by the cone cells and give rise to the electrical messages sent to the visual centers in both the right and left hemispheres of the brain where their blending leads to the sensing of the colors that we see.

The eye has about 137 million of these light-sensitive cells, rods and cones, spread out over the retina. The rods are most numerous in the outermost portion of the retina, which accounts for the fact that we can better detect a faint light, such as a tiny star at night, if we don't look directly at it. The cones are most numerous at a spot in the center of the retina called the "yellow spot" or fovea centralis, where the overlying nerve fibers are particularly thin, thus making the image produced by the cornea and lens, which falls at that spot, much clearer. The number of nerve fibers gathered from the 137 million light sensitive cells are reduced to the cable of the optic nerve containing only about one million nerve cells, one third of which carry the messages from the relatively small fovea centralis. At a point only a short distance from the fovea the optic nerve leaves the eye to go to the visual centers of the brain and there are, consequently, no sensing cells at that point so that we have a blind spot on the retina.

Nerve cells, or neurons, are, one might say, an extension of the brain, which, in turn, is made up of a vast collection of billions of interconnected neurons through which electrical waves travel in a distinctive pattern marking our mental reception of data, our response, and our thought processes. The retina, for instance, is a portion of the brain at the back of the eye to process information brought into our bodies by light waves coming through the eye "camera." Other extensions of the brain, the neurons, are found in other parts of our bodies to bring additional information to the brain via the five senses. Imbedded in the skin, for example, are some three to four million nerve cells that are temperature detectors. Thirty thousand of these nerve cells carry messages from the complex mechanism of the ear, which is designed to "feel" sound waves, or vibrations in the atmosphere, to the auditory centers of the brain.

In the ear, too, are other nerve cells that detect the flow of a fluid in the semicircular canals and transmit to the brain information about the movements of the head and the equilibrium of the body. Nerve cells also carry to the brain chemical information from the taste buds on the tongue, soft palate and epiglottis, which detect four basic taste sensations: sweet, sour, salty, and bitter. Various taste buds specialize in these four basic tastes. Those at the tip of the tongue react to sweetness, those toward the back and sides detect the sour taste, others at the tip and near the back taste saltiness, and some away at the back detect bitterness.

More subtle differences in taste or flavor, however, are not detected by the taste buds, but by the olfactory nerves in the nasal passages. These, again, are chemical or "taste" detectors, but are incredibly sensitive. Tiny amounts of gas molecules of odor-producing substances are mixed with the air that flows past the olfactory centers in the nasal passages. These, in humans are only about the size of a dime. Here the odor-producing substances are first dissolved in the mucus secreted by the nasal membranes, and then are tasted by these chemical-detecting nerve cells. Unlike the eye, ear, and tongue, which respond only to a precise range of stimuli, the olfactory centers are able to respond to a virtually unlimited number of different molecules.

Thus, through the various avenues of the five senses, which we have discovered are actually more than five, our brain, a mass of more than twelve billion neurons, keeps in touch with what is going on in the world around us, and stores away in our memories an abundant wealth of information to help us in dealing with it.

But how accurate is the mind in its concepts and understanding of the real world? "Seeing is believing," we sometimes say, but the eye, or rather the visual centers of our brains, can be fooled. There are such things as optical illusions, and scores of entertainers in the field of magic, sleight-of-hand, or prestidigitation are able to demonstrate that "the hand is quicker than the eye." The reason for this is the image formed by the visual center of the brain is not necessarily what is actually imparted to the eye, but, rather, our mental interpretation of that message. In our seeing, in other words, we have a number of assumptions or preconceptions derived from our experience, or learning, that help to determine what we see.

What our eyes actually detect, as noted above, is energy to which their retinas are especially sensitive. This energy, according to modern physics, comes to the eye, or any other detecting mechanism, in the form of little bundles, or quanta, of energy called photons. These photons travel at the rate of 299,792.5 km/second (186,282 mi./sec.) through the universe (or space) from their source to target. This is the ultimate speed limit in nature. The source of by far the largest number of these quanta to enter the receptors of our eyes is the Sun. It takes them about 8 minutes, 13.2 seconds, on average, to make that nearly 93-million-mile journey. Rarely, however, are they permitted to enter our eyes directly from that source. So intense is the light of the Sun, so massive the amount of energy that it emits, that, even at such a distance, looking directly at it would overload the nerve cells in our retinas and soon destroy them. Therefore the light that comes to the eye is largely indirect, reflected or refracted, and considerably modified in the process. Because of the refraction, the sky, during daylight, is blue. Clouds reflect, obscure, or disperse some of the light from the Sun. But when that light falls directly or indirectly upon some non-white object, some wavelengths of the energy are absorbed by it, and others, unless it is totally black, are reflected. We see the remaining wavelengths, which our eyes perceive as colors. At night the Moon and the planets other than Earth shed reflected sunlight on our world. Other light that we can see is indirect sunlight in the sense that it is energy from the Sun that has been stored in one way or another and then released to give us light and heat. This is true of the fossil fuels that can be burned, or the electricity, that is derived, most often, from stored fossil fuel energy as well. The stars, which are other suns, supply a bit of light energy, but they are so far away that the amount is infinitesimal.

There is, however, in recent times a source of non-solar energy that is coming to have some prominence in our world. This is nuclear energy, derived from the fusion or fission of the atoms that go to make up all matter. This is the same kind of energy that powers the Sun itself, which is a huge nuclear reactor of the fusion type. All atoms disintegrate at a slower or faster rate, and, sometimes, they also merge. In both cases they release energy in the process. Human ingenuity has discovered how, in certain instances, to speed up this process and release massive amounts of such energy either for destruction, as in nuclear weapons, or for constructive work.

In most cases the emission of nuclear energy is so slow and unobtrusive as to escape detection by our senses, though geophysicists believe that a considerable amount of the heat energy that melts the inner core of the earth and its mantle comes from the disintegration of radioactive elements therein. The crust and mantle are good insulators so that not too much of this interior heat gets to the surface except in volcanic activity, hot springs, and geysers. Some of the red hot lava, of course, emits visible radiation and may have been one way in which the earliest humans became acquainted with fire and its properties. Largely, however, this form of nonsolar energy is in the range of infrared or heat radiation, which is detected most readily by the temperature-sensing nerve cells in the skin.

Light, or visible radiation, is only one small part of a wide range of electromagnetic energy. Light varies between four and eight ten thousandths of a millimeter in wavelength, with violet light being the shortest in wavelength (0.4—0.422 microns) and red being the longest (0.647—0.8 microns). This doubling of the wavelength, 4/10 to 8/10 microns, constitutes an octave in the spectrum, and electromagnetic radiation totals more than sixty octaves. Cosmic rays, at the lower end of this energy spectrum, are five hundred billionths of a millimeter in wavelength, while the longest radio waves are more than twenty kilometers. Scientists have given many different names to various parts of this energy spectrum. The shortest in wavelength and highest in energy are the cosmic rays, then gamma rays, x-rays, ultraviolet, visible light of the various rainbow colors violet through red, then infrared, microwaves, short radio waves and long radio waves. Beyond even these there have been discovered, recently, very long micro-pulsations reaching millions of kilometers in length.

The eye, as we have noted, is sensitive to only a narrow range of these energy waves: those that alter the chemistry of certain substances in the retina. Nerve cells in the skin are able to detect some of the infrared or heat radiation. They cannot detect the ultraviolet or x-rays and other short wavelengths though these have the potential to destroy cells. Ordinarily radio waves are also undetectable by our senses, but humans have had the ingenuity to build instruments to generate and modify radio waves in either their amplitude or frequency, and other instruments to detect these modifications and translate them back into sounds or even pictures via radio and TV. Even some that we cannot detect directly by our senses, like microwaves or x-rays, we can harness to work for us.

What Do We Know and How Do We Know It?

In what has been said above about light, there has been a basic contradiction. At first light is referred to as little bundles, or quanta, of energy. Later on much appears about "energy waves" and "wavelengths." What is light, then? Is it particles or waves? The debate over this question has gone on for three centuries. Christaan Huygens, a Dutch-born mathematician and astronomer, published his Treatise on Light in 1690, wherein he theorized that light, like sound, consisted of wave motion. Sound, of course, consisted of compression waves in air. But light travels through a vacuum. In what medium were its waves carried then? Huygens postulated an ether, something that was invisible, weightless, and otherwise undetectable. This ether pervaded the universe, obviously, since light traveled from the distant stars to the Earth.

Sir Isaac Newton took the opposing view. Light, unlike sound, did not bend around corners, he argued. It traveled only in a straight line. Therefore it was corpuscular in nature, a stream of minute particles.

Nearly a century later Thomas Hardy showed experimentally, in the phenomenon of interference, that light was definitely wavelike in nature. The explanation of diffraction, which had been observed even by Newton, showed that it could travel around corners, too. The reason that it does not do so as readily as sound waves is because of a much shorter wavelength. Further studies and experimentation by scientists, such as Fresnel and Foucalt in the nineteenth century, firmly established the wave theory of light. Faraday, Maxwell, Hertz, and Marconi showed that this theory also applied to other forms of electromagnetic radiation, such as radio waves, heat radiation, ultraviolet, x-rays, and gamma rays. All were apparently transmitted as fast traveling waves in the universal medium of the ether.

Then, at the beginning of the twentieth century, along came young Albert Einstein who proved, mathematically, that the ether did not exist! At the same time he showed that light, in order to displace electrons from light-sensitive metal in the photoelectric phenomenon, had to be in the form of discrete quanta of energy, now identified as photons (light particles). Five years earlier a fellow German physicist, Max Planck, had given mathematical evidence to support the view that all electromagnetic energy came in the form of tiny bundles called quanta. These vary in the amount of energy they carry depending on their wavelength: the shorter wavelengths representing the greater energy. Further development of this quantum theory by Planck, deBroglie, Schroedinger, Heisenberg, and others added to the evidence that electromagnetic energy was somehow both particles and waves, as contradictory as this might seem. Both Huygens and Newton had been right, and both had been wrong!

To give expression to the seemingly contradictory relationship of these energy particles and their frequency or wavelength, Dr. Planck evolved the formula: $E = hv$, where E is the energy content of the quantum, v is the frequency of the wave involved, and h is a new constant of physics called, appropriately, Planck's Constant. The value of h was worked out to be 6.625×10^{-27}, or 6,625 preceded by a decimal point and 26 zeros!

The similarity of this formula, dealing with the infinitesimal quantities of energy in the tiny quanta, to $E = mc^2$, that of Einstein dealing with the immense quantities of energy in matter, is obvious. Planck's Constant, h, and the constant of the speed of light, c, as used in Einstein's formula, are two universal constants, the implications of which have revolutionized modern physics.

For example, in 1925 the French physicist, Louis de Broglie, explained the relationship between matter and radiation by suggesting that electrons, too, were not simply particles, but wave systems. An electron's wavelength, lambda, is equivalent to h/mn, where h is Planck's Constant, m is the mass of the particle, and v is its velocity. Subsequent investigation indicated that,

What Do We Know and How Do We Know It?

not only electrons, but protons, neutrons, whole atoms, and even molecules have wavelengths. The atom in the new physics becomes a related system of waves of energy. The waves themselves become waves of probability in mathematical terms. We can picture ourselves, therefore, as living in a universe of wave particles, or, as one scientist facetiously put it, "a universe of wavicles." All material things are both particles and waves at the same time. Yet, because of the exceedingly small quantity of Planck's Constant, above, the waves associated with things of ordinary size are almost negligible. Only when we are dealing with very small material objects, such as electrons, does the wave aspect assume a more important part in our understanding of what is taking place. Physicists then look upon it as only a probability that an electron will be at a certain place at a definite time. This introduces an element of uncertainty into basic Physics, which Werner Heisenberg presented in 1927 as the "Uncertainty Principle" in nuclear physics theory.

Max Planck, who had conceived the quantum theory and announced it in 1900, described the change in the concepts of mechanics by saying it is no more true to describe the relationship of sub-atomic particles in ordinary physical terms than it would be to take a microscopic study of a painting to obtain a clear picture of its meaning. Even so, one cannot get an adequate picture of the laws of nature, without regarding the whole picture.[3]

In short, what all this means is that in modern physics the immutable natural laws that we once thought pervaded and controlled all nature are ultimately based on uncertainty, and that cause and effect, once so idolized in the sciences as the key to all natural phenomena, are ultimately dependent upon the mathematical formulae of probability. It is also interesting to note that Christaan Huygens, who introduced the speculation that led, finally, to this viewpoint of modern physics, also, in 1657, worked out some of the basic mathematics of the theory of probability

15

that plays so essential a role in it!

We must conclude from all this that the reality of the world out there is quite different from what it appears to our minds to be through the medium of our senses. And yet scientists have faith (akin to the religious variety) that leads them to affirm that our minds can apprehend and comprehend that reality.

Summing up the part that the human mind has in correlating our sense impressions and applying them to the world around us, Gerald Holton gives it as Albert Einstein's viewpoint that, "Reality is a relation between what is in you and outside of you."

In other words it was Einstein's view that order in our sense impressions is produced by the creation of general concepts, by relations among these concepts, and by relations of some kind between the concepts and our sense experience. It is by this process that the world of our sense experience becomes comprehensible. He said, "One could say that the eternally incomprehensible thing about our world is its comprehensibility."[4]

Perhaps the best way to express our present-day understanding of epistemology (the science of how we know things) is to say that we live in a universe made up of complex relationships, and our minds, being an exceedingly complex relationship of nerve cells in the brain, have developed the capacity to perceive and understand those relationships.

A relatively new approach in the science of psychology has attempted to study the characteristics of our sense perceptions and how the mind interprets them. This is the Gestalt Psychology advanced by a number of German-American psychology professors, Max Wertheimer, Kurt Koffka, and Wolfgang Kohler. Its approach to the understanding of the operation of the senses and the mind's perception of the world around it is to see our mental processes as responding not so much to isolated stimuli as to patterns, organized groupings, and configurations (Gestalt theory is sometimes called configurationism). The original meaning of the

German word, *gestalt*, is form, figure, shape, or structure, but this meaning is extended by Gestalt Psychology to embrace extended qualities perceived in organized entities.[5]

In short what it says is that our brains, through their sensory extensions, perceive relationships. The individual stimuli of neurons in our nervous system are not perceived in isolation, but in relationship to what other neurons are receiving, so that we see an object as a whole, together with its relationship to surrounding objects and/or background. We also hear a particular vibration from a sound source not in isolation, but in relationship to a pattern of sound, be it a roll of thunder, a musical melody or harmony, or a spoken series of sounds that form words and sentences. Our other senses, likewise, provide data such as texture, coldness, or warmth detected by temperature-sensitive nerve endings, the taste and odor as well as the warmth of a cup of coffee, for example, or the pungent odor that is associated with a little black animal, about the size of a domestic cat, with broad white stripes down its back. A baby senses the whole pattern of facial features, a gentle, comforting touch, a feeling of security, a source of the satisfaction of hunger pangs, and a pleasant, lulling voice that become the whole series of interrelated experiences of mother, long before it has learned the words "mamma" or "mom", which label and communicate that complex pattern of relationships.

Even our memories, it seems, as little understood as this aspect of our mental processes remains, are stimulated by various associations or relationships. Struggling to recall the name of a place or a person we go back through our memories searching for some associations with that place or person, and, as often as not, the name we seek will suddenly come to our consciousness.

The whole process of remembering or recalling some sensory experience (or, more particularly, our mental interpretation of that experience) has been investigated in the new and rapidly developing cognitive science. This is a discipline that uses the latest discoveries in a number of related fields, such as the anatomy of the human brain and nervous system, biology, psychology, behavior and language studies, and even computer science, to develop a scientific picture of how our minds develop and operate.

Examining various alternative explanations of how the mind stores and catalogues up to one hundred trillion bits of information during an average human lifetime, cognitive scientists conclude that the brain is an information processing system. How this works has been described by Morton Hunt in his book, The Universe Within.[6]

It all begins, as we have previously seen, with the input of the various senses that translate light quanta, sound waves, sensations from the taste buds, olfactory centers, the nerves sensitive to touch and temperature in the skin, etc., into electrical impulses traveling through the neural network. Almost instantly they are carried to centers in the brain that are called sensory buffers. Here they are held briefly until we can pay attention to them. Much more data arrive in these centers than we can deal with, but it is held there long enough for us to somehow select what we want give attention to even after the event that caused the sensory experience has ceased. What is thus held briefly in these sensory buffers constitutes a very short-term memory, holding data only a few seconds at the most.

Just what it is in our brains that selects to which of these sensations we pay attention, and thus process further, the cognitive scientists cannot say. Apparently this is some function of the organism as a whole, a response of the complex relationships that make us up. We can call it the self, the conscious mind, the ego, or some other label, but just how it works to make its selections we cannot tell. Sometimes, of course, as in lower forms of life, it reacts to warning sensations and responds defensively to protect the organism. Other times the selection is on the much subtler basis

18

nitive scientists believe that the right hemisphere of
ributes to what we call spiritual sensitivity, flashes
etic or mystical inspiration, inductive reasoning,
erception of less than obvious relationships. An
this kind of brain functioning is to be seen in the
iscovery of the concept of specific gravity by the
ematician, Archimedes (c. 287—212 B.C.E.).
this tale, the king of Syracuse asked Archimedes to
ether a gold crown that had been made for him was
old. The scientist, however, was instructed not to
own in any way in testing it. The problem puzzled
reatly, and he spent much time in thinking about it
when he was about to take a bath. As he stepped
ub of water he noted that it overflowed, and, in a
it, he saw that the volume of water that overflowed
the volume of the body immersed in the tub.
principle to the king's crown, he reasoned that if
it in a vessel of water and noted the volume of fluid
ced, he could compare that with the volume dis-
equal weight of pure gold and thus determine
d an admixture of less dense metal. So thrilled was
by this sudden insight, tradition tells us, that he
the bath and ran naked through the streets toward
outing, "Eureka, Eureka!" ("I have it!) We may well
it was the right hemisphere of Archimedes' brain
the visual perception that related the volume of the
volume of displaced water.
o attribute to the right hemisphere of the brain the
r dreams, especially those taking place during the
ep sleep, when they are less likely to involve lan-
lism. And, by association, to the right side of the
attributed the hidden perceptions and/or memo-
Sigmund Freud gave the label, the Unconscious

of desires, value systems, long-range purposes, or other criteria of
which we may or may not be conscious.

As soon, however, as we give attention to some of these sensory impressions in the buffer, we begin to process them further.
We relate them to other information we have, sensory experiences we have had previously, and transform them into meaningful symbols, often into words that we can process more easily. Those sensations to which we do not give attention quickly
decay and are lost to our memory. To retain for longer periods the
data in the short-term memory we either have to rehearse them
for a time, or subject them to the process of further thinking.
Rehearsal, for example, is what we do with a telephone number
between the time we look it up in the directory and dial it. Or it
is what the schoolchild does with the poem he or she has been
required to learn, or the actor does with his lines. We run through
it, again and again, to make sure that it lodges in our memory at
least until we need to use it.

Rehearsal, by itself, does not make any changes in the data
that go into the short-term memory. But to go into the long-term
memory sensory data is transformed by what the cognitive scientists call elaborative processes into a form that can be and is
filed in the long-term memory. Elaborative processes consist in
giving thought to the data in order to classify them, looking for
patterns, associations, groupings, the grasping of deeper meanings from images, words, sentences, together with a context or
background of previously acquired knowledge, and classifying
those meanings or linking them to other information in our long-
term memories. This can take place very quickly, as, for example,
when we read or hear a sentence and grasp its meaning even
though we could not repeat it verbatim.

In the long-term memory, itself, new information, as interpreted and classified, is tied in with various bits of related information in a semantic network. This, of course, is what is done

with various bits of information in the memory of a computer. However, a study of this memory process indicates that although remembered information is categorized by subject matter to some extent, the arrangement is far less orderly and regular than the categories in the computer memory, or a library card catalogue, for example. We have more redundant ways of retrieving information from our long-term memories, and often have all sorts of non-logical or even non-meaningful clues associated with it that help us retrieve it from seemingly irrelevant associations.

Cognitive scientists are also aware that there is some sensory information that passes directly from the sensory buffers into the long-term memory without going through the stages of rehearsal or elaborative processing. This is what happens, for instance, when we recognize a face, an object or a melody without being aware of paying attention to them or thinking about them. As a matter of fact scientists have now found evidence that the left and right hemispheres of the human brain differ in the way in which they process the sensory information that comes to them. Much of this evidence has been derived from a study of what happens when a person has suffered a lesion that destroys some of the neural network in the brain. Accidents or strokes affecting primarily the left hemisphere of the neocortex are characterized by an impairment in speech, writing ability, and mathematical problem solving. Those taking place in the right hemisphere, however, result in an impairment of three-dimensional vision, pattern recognition, musical ability, and the formation of nonverbal concepts. More recently the evidence of specialization by the right and left hemispheres of the brain have been confirmed by the study of patients who have undergone surgical treatment for severe cases of grand-mal epilepsy. The treatment has been to surgically sever the corpus collosum, a large cable of nerve fibers, which connects the left and right hemispheres and evidently serves the purpose of feeding information back and forth

between them. Superficially th
effect on the mentality of the pa
to the success of the operation in
dramatically. Careful experime
that communication between t
cut, and their functioning se
These showed, for example, th
more competent in recognizing
the right side was better at re
metrical figures. Indeed the spe
the neocortex have been determ
speech, reading, writing, verba
categorizing, musical performa
ing more than one thing at a t
detail in drawings; Right brain
facial recognition, visual space
way," visual closure, musical
tions, and achieve proper form

Thus, it would seem, the r
the kinds of functions noted
recognition of patterns, forms
The brain's left hemisphere, c
labeling, classifying, arrangin
ing data in the long-term me
they can be retrieved, when v
the minds of other persons.

There is memory connec
hemisphere, too, of course, b
and related to other informat
any conscious effort on our
know as feelings and intuitio
nicated to other minds exce
enough to grasp from our en

Son
the brai
of insig
and/or
illustrat
story of
Greek
Accordi
determir
really pu
damage
Archime
until one
into the
flash of ir
was equa
Applying
he immer
that it dis
placed by
whether i
Archimed
dashed ou
the palace
assume th
that provic
crown to t

Some
control of
periods of
guage sym
brain may
ries to whi

Mind. When these were embarrassing or painful, the left side of the brain, which prepared one's thoughts to be communicated to others, repressed the unpleasant details or sublimated them into a more socially acceptable outward expression. Since it is true that we think consciously in the symbolism of words, the non-verbal memories of the right side of our brains do become, essentially, sub- or unconscious in nature. Hence, in Freudian terms, the verbal-thinking side of our brains is the ego and super-ego (reason) which monitors, reinterprets and sometimes censors or represses the perceptions of the right brain which, in a less satisfactory manner, corresponds to the id. Actually the Freudian id embraces not only the right cerebral hemisphere, but, possibly even more specifically, the basic animal brain in which are centered such responses as aggressive or amorous behavior.

Students of the evolution of the brain see a tripartite structure in it corresponding to various evolutionary stages: the reptilian brain, or R-complex; the limbic system, a mammalian development characterized by emotional responses; and, finally, the neo-cortex, which developed in the primate family. Freud made a distinction between the preconscious, wherein resided the nonverbal memories, and the unconscious which he saw as a repository for the repressed thoughts that were not allowed the light of conscious expression by the ego or superego. Brain anatomy and its evolutionary development, however, give a more complex model of the mental apparatus than does Freud's layered look.

There are those who seek some evidence in the brain's structure and functioning for such phenomena as extrasensory perception, precognition, and spiritualistic communication. So far, however, a detailed scientific study of the brain's cellular structure and neurological patterns, as well as use of the most sensitive radio wave receivers, reveal no such circuitry or radiation. It is, to be sure, not impossible that the basically microelectrical circuits in the brain's vast store of neurons could be sensitive to and pick up electromagnetic waves beamed out from similar circuits in other brains as a kind of natural shortwave radio system. But until evidence is found for such a structure or function somewhere within the neural network, that possibility must remain a mere speculation, and evidence for it must become much more positive than the occasional, coincidental and vague "feelings" that are cited for it up to now. The same, perhaps more regretfully, must also apply to those theories of a supernatural revelation or inspiration that many in the religious community hold to as a source of absolute truth. The sure scientific evidence for such a phenomenon is missing.

Revelation, as opposed to reason (i.e., the process of thinking), in the conventional theology, is probably not, as usually assumed, the imparting of ready-made knowledge from a divine or supernatural source. Far more likely it is simply the perception of relationships by the right hemispheres of our brains, the source of which remains mysterious to the symbolic thinking and verbal expression of our left cerebral hemispheres.

Since our attention, in this chapter, has been primarily directed to the process by which we acquire and store knowledge, there remains yet another aspect of the brain's function, which we have thus far neglected. This is its role as a behavior-producing organ. This may well be regarded as its primary function. At least that branch of psychology professionals who are called Behaviorists consider it to be the most important and devote their time to the study of how the animals, including man, behave as an indication of how their minds work. To be sure the normal functioning of the most primitive brains or neural networks was to produce behavior; either of a defensive kind to preserve the organism, or to satisfy its basic inner urges to feed and reproduce. So the primitive single-celled creature, the amoeba, will move away from the light that penetrates the surface of the waters in which it dwells, probably because this takes it into shadows or crevices where it is more hidden from the higher organisms that want to eat it. On the other hand, a plant, which requires light for its metabolism, will grow toward a light source and turn its leaves broadside to the direction from which the light is coming so as to more efficiently absorb the incoming energy. Yet the plant does not even have a nervous system! Apparently its cells have a built-in or instinctive response to the light, which reflects in the plant's behavior. Or an insect, such as a moth, may have an instinctive response in its neural makeup that causes it to fly toward a light, such as a candle, even though getting too close will kill it. This is not necessarily stupid behavior, as we might sardonically assume, since for hundreds of millions of years this behavior was beneficial to the insect until man came along with his artificial light sources that made it fatal. Unfortunately, an evolutionary developed brain trait cannot be quickly modified by the moth to suit it to a changed situation. But if we characterize its behavior as stupid, what about that of human beings who will continually court the dangers of ingesting alcohol, tobacco smoke, and hallucinogenic drugs, even though smart enough to know that this behavior will severely impair or kill them? What's more we are able to modify our response to the danger much more quickly since it is learned and not instinctive behavior.

As is true for much more primitive organisms, with their less complex neural systems, a great deal of our human behavior is automatic. Thus we do not take thought each time we take a breath, saying to ourselves: "I must expand my lungs and inhale or collapse them partially and exhale." That all goes on automatically without our consciously thinking about it, although we can consciously modify it to breathe faster or deeper, or even hold our breath for a time. Other automatic responses include opening the iris of the eye to expand the pupil and admit more light; or closing it to reduce the light; secreting saliva in our mouths, especially when we think of our favorite food, or when we smell it; producing sweat from our pores to maintain a cooler body temperature when exercising vigorously or encountering a hot summer day; digesting our food; altering our heartbeat to meet the need for more oxygen in various body parts; or causing our glands to produce more or less of certain chemicals to maintain a sensitive chemical balance in our bodies. Even simply standing in one place and maintaining our balance on two feet requires continual automatic bodily adjustments. If we had to give conscious thought to each of these and many other kinds of behavior, we probably could never think of anything else. So we have subconscious brain centers and ganglia, or neuron complexes, in other parts of the body, which are parts of the autonomic (self-controlled or involuntary) nerve system. Autonomic and automatic are not necessarily synonymous in this connection, but the autonomic system, through its divisions, the sympathetic and parasympathetic, govern most automatic bodily activities. The sympathetic system, so called because it responds to the body's feelings and/or pains, often initiates a bodily response to that call for help. The parasympathetic system exists to countermand and thus to control the responses called for by the sympathetic system. Between the two of them they regulate bodily behavior that is not consciously controlled.

And yet, as indicated, at least some of the actions and reactions initiated and controlled by the autonomic nerve system can be modified or altered by the conscious mind. Even more of these can be brought under control through the techniques of biofeedback recently developed. This consists of the use of various continually acting measurement devices to indicate the autonomic response, and then learning what thoughts or conscious decisions will alter that response.

All this leads us to the more fundamental question of how

the conscious mind influences our behavior. What happens in our brain when we decide to do or not do something? The answers to such questions remain obscure at best in spite of our intensive study of brain activity. As noted back when we were considering the brain's selection of data to process for storage in the long-term memory, there may be some holistic function of the brain which gives it decision-making powers. Again we can call it the self, the conscious mind, the ego, or even the soul, but how it works we do not know.

Dr. A. Campbell Garnett, who was the professor in a number of courses in the Philosophy of Religion that I took as a student at the University of Wisconsin, had a theory that both the human soul and God were to be found in this mental phenomenon of the will. "Personality is a system of will," he wrote, equating it with the soul of religious doctrine, and the mental act of awareness observed by the psychologists.[7] "God in us," an immanent deity, is the altruistic or disinterested will to the greatest good of all concerned. Though God, in this sense, was revealed in history and in the Person of Jesus Christ, it is to be doubted that He corresponds with the Creator God of the Christian faith, for if, as modern biology teaches, man did not evolve until the last two million to 600,000 years ago (there is disagreement among many paleoanthropologists as to which of several anthropoid species were human and which were prehuman), then we wonder where God was and what He was doing in the previous thirteen and a half billion years since the time of the Big Bang formation of the Universe.

This big question of where our traditional idea of God fits into the pattern of knowledge about the universe around us and our understanding of it is, then, the topic of the next chapter in our study.

[1] Ecclesiastes 12:12.

[2] They are about forty times larger in dogs, for instance, indicating the higher dependence on smell in certain animal species.

[3] 'The Universe in the Light of Modern Physics," The Great Ideas of Today" (1962) Chicago, Encyclopedia Brittanica, pp. 487-499.

[4] Einstein, (1979) A Centenary Volume Cambridge, MA, Harvard University Press, p.158.

[5] Wolfgang Kohler, (1947) Gestalt Psychology, New York, Mentor Books, esp. Chapter 6.

[6] Morton Hunt, (1982) The Universe Within New York: Simon and Schuster, pp. 84ff.

[7] A.C. Garnett, (1942) A Realistic Philosophy of Religion, Chicago, Willet Clark & Co., pp.237 ff.

CHAPTER TWO

"WHERE IS GOD?"

"God is relationship."[1]

In the well-known lines by Robert Browning, found in his poem, "Pippa Passes":

> God's in his heaven
> All's right with the world!

But since, in the world of the late-twentieth century, the last clause of this affirmation is so obviously wrong we may be led to question the first part as well. Such a conclusion may indeed have been questionable in the world of the nineteenth century, when Browning wrote it, if someone had added up all the social and environmental conditions around the world, though it may be that the exuberant and innocent young working girl, Pippa, who sings the song, would never have thought to do that. Yet the premise here has always been wrong. Heaven, as a place, does not exist, and never has. It may exist to some as a hope or an ideal, but even that is probably unrealistic. Mostly the idea of heaven is a concept derived from a primitive, prescientific, and mistaken cosmology, and from the typical, possibly metaphorical, biblical terminology that reflects that cosmology.

In the belief of most of the people of the Middle East in Bible times the earth was a bowl-shaped or relatively flat disk or, sometimes, a rectangular strip of land, surrounded by mountains, on which rested a firmament, a dome-shaped expanse or vault, sometimes pictured as being like a curtain or a tent, and at other times more like a burnished metal dome. The earth or dry land was intersected by rivers, and dotted with hills, valleys, lakes, and seas. Outside of the mountain "pillars of heaven" was another great river or sea, surrounding the earth, and, beneath everything, a "great deep" or watery abyss. In some unspecified manner the earth or dry land rested on pillars in this vast area of the "waters under the earth." Above the heavenly dome, too, there was another expanse of waters from which rain came down through the windows or gates that were sometimes opened in the firmament. There, too, were the storehouses of hail and snow ready to be dropped through the "windows of heaven" upon the earth beneath. The Sun, Moon, and stars were lights hung by God in the sky or firmament to "mark times and seasons," and "to separate day from night." Within or beneath the surface of the earth was the realm of the dead called Sheol, and there dwelt the "shades" of deceased humanity.[2]

The New Testament gives no cosmological picture corresponding to this, but, in spite of having been exposed, possibly, to the less mystical, more rational, ideas of the Greeks in this as in other areas, its authors seem to have basically retained the older Hebrew concepts.[3] In Old Testament times the "heavens" were nearly always spoken of in the plural, and the New Testament mentions several levels in heaven, with God dwelling in the highest one. Such an earth-centered cosmology, accepted uncritically in Bible times, has now, obviously, been superseded by modern astronomy's concept of a vast universe where the Earth is a small planet of a medium-sized star, in one branch of a minor galaxy, floating in a vast ocean of space-time, which is lightly sprinkled with perhaps as many as a hundred billion galaxies! This turning away from the concept of an earth-centered cosmology, which began with the observations of Copernicus and Galileo, and has literally exploded in terms of stars and galaxies with twentieth century astronomy advanced by such persons as Slipher, De Sitter, Hubble, Humanson, and Shapley, is probably the greatest of all the revolutions wrought by science in human thought. It, even more than the idea of evolution, has caused much of the biblical language and its thought forms to become outmoded.

To be sure, we still use that language, especially in religious circles, but we use it metaphorically. Some of the early Russian cosmonauts sought to ridicule this religious language by announcing that they didn't find any God sitting up there above the clouds in outer space. We laughed at their stupidity in taking that metaphorical language literally and expecting that they would see God "in the flesh," as it were. Even though, in shocking familiarity, some superficially religious people also speak lightly of "the man upstairs," we know that, though the majesty of God's creation is to be seen in the stars, the planets, and the wheeling galaxies, God, Himself, is not to be found there. Where, then, is God?

Actually, the concept of a heavenly deity or sky god was an advance over even more primitive theological views. Humanity, it seems, found its earliest gods much closer to home in earthly surroundings. What the first concepts of deity were is lost in the mists of antiquity, and even such clues as we have are subject to a wide variety of interpretations and all conclusions are largely speculative.

However, the first indications we have discovered of a religious consciousness and practice were among the immediate hominid predecessors of modern man, the Neanderthals. This earliest variety of the species to which we belong, *homo sapiens*, flourished nearly 120 millennia, from about 150,000 to 32,000 years ago. That is nearly four times as long as modern man has been on the scene. In caves that were occupied by Neanderthals in central Europe there are indications that a cave bear cult was practiced, and skulls and leg bones of these huge animals were set up in what appears to have been shrine-like arrangements in the deep interior of those natural shelters. The cave bear was as much as nine feet tall, standing on its hind legs, and much larger than a grizzly, but so fascinated were the Neanderthal hunters with these animals of great fierceness and power that they apparently hunted them to near extinction. In one cave a stone chest containing thirty cave bear skulls was found! The Clan of the Cave Bear, a modern, best-selling novel by Jean Auel, appearing in both hardcover and paperback editions, gives us an imaginative account of what the religious rites may have been like that took place around such objects in Neanderthal caves.[4]

Such is the survival potential of religious activities that rites involving bears lasted into comparatively recent times among the hunting peoples of northern Europe: Laplanders, Siberian tribes, and Eskimos in the arctic wilds of the American continent. Rituals involving bears are even still to be found among the Ainu of northern Japan.

Still another indication of religious thought and spiritual interests among the Neanderthals is the evidence that they frequently buried their dead with ceremony, placing animal bones and stone weapons and tools in the graves with them, and having cemetery areas in or near some of their caves. In one cave in Iraq, the study of the soil around such graves gave evidence from pollen levels that they even decorated the graves with flowers!

While the Neanderthals seemingly worshiped strength and power as manifested in the species, Ursus spelacous, their more modern successors, the Cro-Magnons, who appeared in various locations some thirty to forty thousand years ago, may have considered sacred the mystery of reproduction and fertility. Among the utilitarian stone tools and weapons they left behind in their cave habitations has also been found a widespread figurine carved from stone: that of a voluptuous female figure, with exaggerated breasts, wide hips, and large buttocks, which suggests the idea of an "earth mother" or fertility goddess. If, as seems likely, this was some sort of female idol or fertility symbol, it heralded a form of religion that also has lasted into comparatively recent times. Among the idols that the seventh and eighth century, B.C.E., Hebrew prophets denounced in their sermons were those of the Baalim and Ashtaroth, pagan fertility gods, whose licentious rites the average male Israelite evidently found attractive. Other primitive peoples around the world plainly had similar deities representing both the fertility of the earth as well as domestic or hunted animals and human beings.

The modern man species, Cro-Magnon, was also skillful at, and deeply interested in, the art of painting, as evidenced by the numerous paintings of animals and abstract forms on the walls of European caves, particularly in southwestern France and northern Spain. These paintings, especially those that are believed to have been made from about 25,000 down to 10,000 B.C.E., are vivid, vibrant, and exceedingly lifelike, capturing the characteristics and realistic poses of animals and, occasionally human figures, in a remarkable way that has seldom been equaled in more recent art. The location of such murals, and sometimes bas-relief sculptures, in quite inaccessible areas of many of the caves suggests to some archaeologists a ceremonial purpose, perhaps religious in nature, and associated, many believe, with initiation ceremonies for youth reaching manhood or womanhood. At the very least these astonishing cave paintings indicate a cultural advance in the primitive human species in its dedication of more time and energy toward artistic pursuits, and a remarkable closeness to the world of nature that surrounded them.

Later on, in the latter stages of the New Stone Age, about 5,000 B.C.E., and lasting into the early Bronze Age, about 2,800 B.C.E., (i.e., the beginning of Stonehenge on the Salisbury Plain in England), prehistoric peoples of Europe built vast monuments of stone. Whether these served a religious purpose as temples, or a scientific one as observatories, is argued back and forth by archaeologists. Quite possibly they served as both. A careful study of Stonehenge and similar monumental stoneworks both in England and on the continent has shown that they were arranged, at least sometimes, to measure the Sun's apparent advance to its zenith at the beginning of summer and back to its nadir at the beginning of winter. There are also indications that lunar cycles and the rising and setting of some of the more notable stars and planets were also measured. But along with this astronomical use, the structures may also have served as centers of religious ritual for a people whose livelihood depended so much on the rotation of the seasons.

As humanity advanced toward historical times, religion, like language, became more complex. When we arrive at the level of recorded history, at various times in different locations (e.g., 3500 B.C.E. in Mesopotamia; 3100 B.C.E. in Egypt), the catalogue of gods and goddesses as well as the ceremonies for honoring and placating them, were already quite complex. Some of these deities represented in, or were symbolized by, animal figures such as the cat, the jackal, the crocodile, the baboon, the bull and the falcon in Egypt. Others represented phenomena of nature and the cosmos: the sky, the Earth, the Sun, the Moon, mountains, planets (e.g. Mars, Venus), lightning, and thunder. Marduk, who became a chief of all the gods in Babylonia, was originally an agricultural deity symbolizing the powers of the hoe (or cultivation). Later Greek and Roman deities, and those of the Germanic tribes in Europe, can be seen as a blending of the gods and goddesses of the great empires with the native tribal deities having similar powers. In this manner, through the processes of conquest and cultural exchange, pantheons of gods and goddesses were built up, and fads of popular religion developed and declined.

Prior to these theological accretions of great pantheons, anthropologists surmise, there may have prevailed in many human communities a belief in local spirits inhabiting both animate and inanimate things. This primitive religion, animism, which was then still extant among certain isolated societies in the islands of the South Seas and among some tribes of American Indians, was described by the noted nineteenth-century anthropologist, Sir Edward Burnett Tylor. Those in the human societies holding such beliefs, who were recognized as skillful in dealing with such spiritual powers were called shamans, and were the forerunners of the priests of later, more developed faiths. Such shaman-like figures are apparently even portrayed in some of the aforementioned cave paintings of the Cro-Magnons.

Some anthropologists also believe that even prior to the animistic stage of religious belief, there was one called animatism which was that vague, impersonal powers inhabited many natural phenomena. Those powers early man sought to placate or control, depending on whether his rituals were counted to be in the closely related fields of religion or magic.

We may surmise that as humans developed brains capable of self-consciousness and distinguishing between themselves and the world around them, they were often awed or frightened by powers in nature that were greater than their own, such as volcanoes, strong winds, lightning and thunder, animals of great strength or cleverness, or with superhuman abilities such as that of birds to fly, or antelopes to run very fast, or lions, leopards, and tigers to stalk prey. Also, they were undoubtedly impressed with remarkable things such as great trees, waterfalls and springs, the Sun and the Moon; high mountains, volcanoes, deep valleys or canyons and gorges, the dark recesses of caves, the rainbow and the aurora, the fertility of the earth and of young women, and countless other phenomena that often impress us still, even though most of us now know the natural explanation of them.

Some, religionists and scientists alike, consider this to have been a basic belief in the supernatural. This seems however, to be an anachronism. Before there could have been such a conception of the supernatural, there would have to have been a concept of the natural. Some such concept may have been developing among Greek intellectuals several centuries B.C.E., but it hardly seems to have been likely among the masses who followed the popular religions of the day, nor among the Hebrews of biblical times who were more interested in spiritual concepts than scientific ones. It was distinctly not in the thought pattern of most Romans, as practical in engineering and politics as many of them were. Nor did it appear to be in the thinking of the leaders or the general populace in the Holy Roman Empire, whose interest was primarily otherworldly. Not until the Renaissance, and the enlarging interest in nature and science that brought about, did the Western world begin to develop a viewpoint that could be called naturalism, to be contrasted with the older religious doctrines that were based on revelation and supernaturalism. The New Testament, written in the *koine*, or everyday Greek, does have a word, *phusis*, that is often translated as "nature," or, in its adjective form, "natural." This, however, apparently means the characteristics or conditions of human or other life forms. That it is not meant to contrast the worldly with the divine is indicated in II Peter 1:4, which is translated, "partakers of the divine nature." Furthermore, the Greek New Testament, as noted before, has no word for "supernatural." The opposite of "natural" is "spiritual," as indicated in I Corinthians 15: 44, 46. (The same Greek word, *pneumatikos*, is translated "supernatural" in I

Corinthians 10:3-4 by the Revised Standard Version and some other English translations, but this, too, is anachronistic, an attempt to put the New Testament language into more modern thought forms.)

The commonly accepted viewpoint in the societies portrayed in the Judeo-Christian scriptures and other ancient literature was a belief that all things and events were in the hands of the gods or goddesses and an important part of human activity was to learn the means of influencing or winning the favor of their deities. To be sure there were some things and events that were commonplace in their lives, but that did not mean that they were not provided or supported through divine intervention. There were other things and events that were unusual, and these were often described by words that we now translate as "miracles" or "miraculous." The difficulty arises when, because of our modern view that the world is governed by natural law, we consider such miracles to be a suspension of those laws. Scientists, carefully studying the natural world around us, including that vast cosmos of which we are so infinitesimal a part, can find no evidence for such a suspension of nature's laws. Returning to the Bible we find that a more accurate translation of the Hebrew or Greek words that we translate as "miracles," would be "signs" or "wonders." In fact they are often so translated. An exception is the Greek word, *dunamis*, which means "an act or manifestation of power." If the being who acts thus powerfully is regarded as being above nature, as believers commonly do of their deity in the modern world, then, indeed, such beings are supernatural. But, generally, all that such believers really mean is that they are superhuman.

Because of the correlation that arose in our everyday thinking, as natural science developed, between religion and the supernatural, many scientists and other well-educated persons have come to the conclusion that there is little evidence for a supernatural being, and have become either agnostic or atheistic in their views. On the other hand, traditional religious believers often seem to be fighting a retreating battle against the conclusions of modern science. The consequence is that we frequently consider science and religion to be in an adverse relationship, i.e., science vs. religion. This results in an obscurantism in religious circles that impedes the advance of science (knowledge), and a scornful attitude in scientific circles that minimizes and shuns the contributions of religion to our human individual and social well-being. It is the conclusion of this writer, and others of a liberal theological persuasion, therefore, that the conflict situation between religion and science is not likely to improve much, with unhappy consequences for both, until religion gets away from its unbiblical preoccupation with the supernatural.

To return now to the more advanced religions of historical times, we find an increasing tendency to deify impressive natural, but little understood objects in the universe around us. Long before historical times there is ample evidence that human beings had turned their attention to the wonders of the sky, or heavens. The Sun, Moon, known planets and various stars, together with the patterns they made in the night sky, became, in their imagination, the gods and goddesses whom they worshiped. In Egypt, the sky itself was identified as the goddess Nut who stretched her body in an arch over the Earth, which, in their pantheon, was the god, Geb. Each night, according to the mythological explanation, Nut swallowed the sun, the god Re, and each morning he was born again from her loins. In like manner she consumed the stars at dawn and gave birth to them again at night. The cycles observed in the cosmos thus gave rise to the concepts of resurrection and immortality.[5]

Chief among the gods of Egypt was Osiris, son of Geb and Nut. He brought law and order to the Land of the Nile, teaching the Egyptians how to plant and harvest grain, how to survey their fields and lay out boundaries, how to irrigate and harness the annual Nile floods. He taught them how to organize and, as their first king, gave rise to the god-rulers, the Pharaohs. He also ruled the kingdom of the dead, presiding over the judgment of souls and the rewarding of the righteous with immortality. His well-known title was Lord of Everything. Essentially he was a creator god.[6]

In Babylonia a similar role, with only minor differences, was assigned to Marduk, who brought order out of chaos by killing Tiamat, the dragon of the primeval chaos. In early Greek religion the god who occupied much the same position was Zeus, who was known as Jupiter in the Roman pantheon. All three of these deities were symbolized by the planet Jupiter. Other planets represented other gods or goddesses, such as Ishtar, Aphrodite, or Venus by the planet Venus; Nergal (Babylonian), Ares (Greek), and Mars (Roman) by the planet Mars; and Nebo, Hermes, and Mercury by the planet Mercury.[7]

However, not only did the starry heavens provide a habitation for the gods, and hence play a part in the development of humanity's religious thought, but they also were the background for the development of science. The repetitive cycles of the Sun, Moon, planets, and stars led to a sense of order as men and women learned to observe them. As we have noted previously, even as early as the Old Stone Age monumental stone observatories were built. In historic times the pseudo science of astrology was formulated, which led, gradually, to the perfected science of astronomy. The Persian Magi illustrate the former, while the Greek philosophers of the fifth and sixth centuries B.C.E.demonstrate the latter.

Much of the progression in human religious consciousness and conviction is reflected in that depository of the sacred literature of the Hebrew people: the Bible. In the earliest stages of their history as a nomadic people from the deserts of the Middle East, the Hebrews had tribal gods, *elohim* (Ps. 8:5) in the plural, or simply *el* in the singular.

El, or *elohim*, seems to have been a generic name for deity among the Semites, being similar to forms found among the Akkadians, the Phoenecians, and southern Arabs. The derivation is uncertain, but the basic meaning seems to have a relationship to "power" or "might." As well as both the singular and plural forms, it was used frequently in the Hebrew scriptures in combinations, such as El-Elyon (Gen. 14:19), meaning "highest God," the deity worshiped by Melchizedek, the King of Jerusalem in Abraham's time; El Shaddai (Gen. 17:1, 35:11, et al.), the name for the Hebrew deity frequently used during the time of the patriarchs, erroneously translated "God Almighty," but probably meaning "God of the mountain;" El Berith (Judges 9:46) meaning "God of the covenant;" and El Elohe Israel (Gen. 33:19-20), meaning "God, the God of Israel."

El was also frequently a part of Hebrew personal names, such as: Eliezer, Elihu, Eliakim, Elisha, and of course, Elijah, whose name was a combination of two Hebrew words for deity and meant, "Yahweh is my God."

Originally these *elohim*, like the baalim worshiped by the Canaanites, were probably spirits dwelling in various natural phenomena: stones, trees, mountains, springs, etc. An example is found in the story of Jacob's dream of a ladder (or more properly a staircase) reaching up into the sky. Some scholars see the stairway of the dream as a subconscious memory of stories that Jacob had probably heard as a boy about the long stairways leading up the outside of the ziggurats or temple mounds of Babylonia on which processions of priests climbed up and down going to and from the house of the god (temple) on the top. In the story of Jacob's dream (Gen. 28:10-22), the priestly procession is replaced by a procession of angels (messengers or representatives of God) ascending and descending the stairway to heaven. Originally, perhaps, it was the spirits or *elohim* of the place whom Jacob saw in his dream, for he proceeds to call the place "Bethel," i.e., "house of God." About thirty-five years later, returning to the site after his sojourn in the house of Laban in Haran, as a patriarch in his own right, with wives, children, servants and flocks, he established a shrine there that he called, "El Bethel," literally, "the God of the house of God" (Gen. 35:37). The context of the story indicates that he required his family and followers to put away their foreign idols and household deities and thereafter to worship the God of that place, who thus became the tribal deity of the clan of Jacob or Israelites.

A less generic and more personal name for God among the Israelites was YHWH. Some reference to this name for God is found in historic biblical materials prior to the time of Moses (c. 1300 B.C.E.), and it is possible that some of the Hebrew tribes may have used it to refer to their god, but more likely this is a reading back into an earlier time of the later usage. A generally accepted view among Old Testament scholars is that the Israelites acquired this name for their deity during the time they were becoming a more cohesive nation under the leadership of Moses. He, in turn, is thought to have learned the name from the Kenites, a south Arabian Semitic tribe of nomads into which he married after fleeing from Egypt. Their name suggests that they were copper smiths or metal workers. In Exodus, Chapter 3, Moses is pictured as receiving this name for the deity in a special revelation given him at the holy mountain of Sinai through the medium of a desert bush that was on fire but not consumed by the flames. The name, YHWH, is connected in this story to the Hebrew word, *hayah*, meaning "to be." This connection was probably based merely on a similarity in sound. The original meaning, if any, of the Hebrew is now lost in the mists of antiquity. Anyway, as for so many of the earliest gods of mankind, Yahweh was evidently a mountain God.

Creative Relationship

Later, so Exodus tells us, Moses, in response to the commands of this new deity, returned to his own people in Egypt to
rescue them from their slavery there. He led them by long forced
marches back to the sacred mountain of his revelation, and made,
at that place, a covenant, or mutual agreement, between the God,
Yahweh, and the Israelite tribes. But since the Israelites were not
satisfied to dwell in the desert, a means had to be found to assure
the presence of their mountain God with them when they sought
to reenter the land which had been traditionally promised to
their ancestor, Abraham, by his God of the mountain, *El Shaddai*
(Genesis 17:1).

To do this, Moses, possibly making use of the skills of his
wife's tribe, the Kenites, had constructed a box of acacia wood,
decorated with gold plate and figurines, to symbolically house
the deity's power or spirit. They called this box the Ark of the
Covenant, a tangible symbol of that agreement made with their
new God at Sinai, and to provide a shelter for it they raised a tent
(or tabernacle) in which to put it. As described in Exodus, written probably some nine or ten centuries after the events it
depicts, this tabernacle took on many of the characteristics of the
later, more permanent temple of Solomon, which is highly
unlikely. If it existed at all, originally it was probably a much
more simple bedouin shelter, covered with animal skins and
called "the tent of meeting." With this symbolic presence of their
God, the Hebrew tribes eventually (after forty years according to
Exodus) again invaded Palestine, then known as "the land of
Canaan," and wrested possession of some of the higher, less fer-
tile, land from the local inhabitants as their own territory.

The Ark of the Covenant lasted for several centuries, going
through vicissitudes matching the fortunes of the people who
revered it. First Samuel, Chapters 4 thru 7:2, tells how it was captured by the fierce fighters, the Philistines, who installed it in the
temple of their own god, Dagon. There it caused such havoc to

that temple and its idol, as well as being responsible, so they thought, for bringing a bubonic plague upon them, that they loaded it on a wagon drawn by milk cows and sent it back to the Israelites. When David became king, he had the Ark of the Covenant brought to Jerusalem, which he had captured and made into his capital city, and had it set up in a place of honor. Eventually it was housed in the most holy inner room of the temple built by his son, Solomon, where it served as a symbol of Yahweh, Israel's special God.

As the Israelites settled in Palestine and became farmers, the possessors of fields, vineyards, and olive orchards, rather than nomadic shepherds and herdsmen, their desert God also became acclimated to a more settled life and culture. In an age-old historical process called syncretism, which is the merging of diverse cultures and beliefs, the Israelite God, Yahweh, acquired some of the characteristics of the Canaanite baals, and, no doubt, vice versa. As Israel expanded its hold on the Palestinian countryside, and overcame, often slaughtering or expelling, their Canaanite cousins, they took over local shrines and enshrined Yahweh in them. At the same time this fierce and warlike tribal deity of the desert became more and more like a Canaanite Baal, and his worship even took on some of licentious practices that characterized the homage paid to such agricultural deities. The prophets, beginning with Elijah and Elisha, fought against this process, and the accompanying absorption by the Israelites of the Canaanite commercialized culture as opposed to the ancient desert tribesman's hospitality, fair play, and mutual helpfulness. Such prophetic opposition to religious and cultural modification continued on down through the noble diatribes of the writing prophets, Amos, Hosea, Micah, Isaiah, and even Jeremiah. These "troublers of Israel" as they were sometimes called by the rulers of the nation, sought the preservation of the best elements in the old cultural and religious tradition, and the elimination of all the competing customs and rituals of the prevailing idolatry.

Along with the prophet's zeal for religious reform, however, there was also a development in the understanding of the nature and purposes of God. The tribal deity acquired at Sinai and focused, at least symbolically, in a gold decorated wooden box, became a sky God, supreme in the heavens, with a universal power and presence, who was to be worshiped exclusively.[8]

Under the early prophets, Elijah and Elisha, the religion of Israel became a monolatry, i.e. believing that other gods existed but clinging to Yahweh as the one and only God for Israel. Gradually monotheism, a belief in the reality of only one God, developed from this as a theological contribution of the eighth century writing prophets: Amos, Hosea, Micah, and Isaiah. The political vicissitudes of the divided kingdoms of Israel and Judah, situated as they were on the corridor between the perennially great empire of Egypt and those of the middle east, Assyria, Babylonia, and Persia, provided a setting for the development of a world view by these prophets, and an insight into the nature of their God as ruler over not only tiny Palestine, but the larger empires of the known world. God became universal, and exclusive, a single and unrivaled deity.

Ideas of monotheism had appeared in the thinking of some humans centuries earlier, as during the reign of Ikhnaton, a pharaoh of Egypt from about 1375 to 1358 B.C.E. He believed the disk of the Sun in the sky to be the sole god of the universe. But there is no evidence that such philosophical concepts influenced Moses, or the Israelites who followed him out of Egypt, in their beliefs about Yahweh. Not until the time of Deutero-Isaiah, the author of chapters 40 to 55 in the biblical book of Isaiah, can we find the concept of monotheism in the religion of Israel. Genesis 1, which implies it, was written approximately a century later.

Philosophical or theological concepts, however, were not the forte of the eighth-century prophets, whose primary interest was in the moral and ethical behavior of their Israelite contemporaries, and in their loyalty to Israel's God. They contributed to the development of monotheism by their conviction that Yahweh, their God, controlled all nations, i.e., that even their enemies, such as the Assyrians, were His instruments. Their contribution to the evolving concept of God was the insight that He was concerned about human relationships; about justice, integrity, mercy, and love. They began understanding God in terms of relationships.

Jesus, the Nazarene, in the New Testament, inherited and refined the prophets' understanding of God. Like them he did not try to define deity. But, like the people of Bible times in general, he never questioned the existence of God. He assumed it. And, like them, the basic concept of deity underlying his belief was of someone like a super king or emperor, creator and ruler of the universe, who had his throne somewhere above the sky, and a throne room filled with angels who served his will and purposes. Such a concept is reflected in a number of Jesus' parables, and is the one on which his oft-repeated phrase, "the Kingdom of God," was based. On this concept of deity most of the New Testament theology was founded, as most clearly depicted in the final book of the Christian Bible, Revelation. But the main thrust of Jesus' teaching was not in a concept of what God was like, but in His relationship to the world He had created, and especially to mankind. He called God "Father," even, on occasion, using the more intimate term, "Abba," which is somewhat equivalent to "Papa," to express the closeness of that relationship. He compared God's concern and caring for human beings to the concern and care that a good father would have for his children. This was not a particularly new idea in Judaism. Yet Jesus emphasized it more than anyone before him had done. He made it a normal part of people's everyday thinking about God. Also, like the prophets, he emphasized God's righteousness, i.e., His concern for right behavior, integrity, justice, fair play, mercy, and helpfulness.

Creative Relationship

The early Christian literature in the New Testament, including the record of the life and teachings of Jesus in the Gospels, especially the Gospel According to John, and, of course, the letters of Paul of Tarsus, who was a theologian of remarkable reasoning powers, originality, and lucidity, turned much of its attention to concepts of the deity: His purposes and doings. However, the nucleus of Jesus' teaching about the relationships between human beings and their Creator, as well as their proper relationship to one another, remains an integral part of that literature throughout. And it has survived through subsequent centuries, an unforgotten and unforgettable kernel of the true religion of Jesus amid all the controversial and competitive doctrines of the religion about Jesus.

However, there is little room for doubt that after the apostolic age, and the death of the original witnesses to Jesus' life and teachings, Christianity moved more and more to a theological and doctrinal emphasis, showing less concern with the ethical and moral aspects of that teaching. This was due in a large measure to efforts to fight off ideas that were regarded as heresies, i.e., departures from the approved doctrines of the church hierarchy. In many respects this was undoubtedly a good thing, for there was a strong tendency for concepts and practices of the contemporary pagan religions to creep into the Christian faith. This was the same process of syncretism, which had modified Judaism in pre-Christian times, and, in spite of the best efforts of the early Christian leaders to prevent it, the teachings of early Christianity were modified in like manner by these outside influences. The sad and unfortunate part of this historical development, nevertheless, is that it turned the primary emphasis away from Jesus' teachings about relationships to a speculation about his nature and relationship to God. This is reflected in the development of the creeds of Christianity, which from the Apostle's Creed onward to comparatively recent times, dwelt on subtleties of theology and totally ignored Jesus' life and teachings.[9]

As time went on, the energies of Christianity's leaders were directed toward building up the power and prestige of the church, and elaborating its doctrines about God and salvation, rather than in the application of the biblical insights into human relationships to the circumstances of life following the decline of the Roman Empire. Theologies were derived from biblical texts and Church traditions rather than from an understanding of human relationships. Except for some minor Christian sects that arose in the twelfth through seventeenth centuries of the Christian era, the Protestant Reformation did not alter this tendency to any great degree. Primary attention was still paid to theological, soteriological and ritual considerations by Protestant leaders such as Luther, Melancthon, Calvin, Zwingli, and Knox. However, a return to a study of the scriptures, and especially the Gospels, as a source of church authority, could not help but draw more attention to problems of human relationships, and certain Protestant sects, such as the Quakers, Baptists, Unitarians, Methodists, and others did much in the way of developing a social gospel for modern Christianity.

With a further passage of time the problems of individual and group relationships became a major concern in some religious circles. In the twentieth century church leaders and workers, especially in the field of Christian Education, have realized that they need to know something about the sociological phenomena of groups, and their interactions. Thus they have felt the need to study group processes, and to understand group dynamics, disciplines that have in recent times become quite important in the business world and in governmental structures. Though groups have always been important on the human scene in the family, the clan, the tribe, the community, and the state, they have received little scholarly attention until modern times.[10]

Because no person lives entirely in isolation in our modern world, everyone belongs to a number of groups, some unorganized and ill-defined, others highly structured and definite. Among the former might be listed gender: male and female; race; nationality; local community; economic class: such as upper, lower, or middle; occupation: such as a professional person, a laborer, a white-collar or blue-collar worker, or, more specifically, a teacher, a lawyer, a physician, a clergyman, a plumber, a truck driver, and so on. Other such groupings might include religious denominations, political parties, college graduates, commuters, suburbanites, and so on. Maybe even hermits might be considered such a category. The latter, more specific and structured groups, might include the family, our local church, our club or lodge, a board or committee on which we serve, or a shop or office in which we work. For most, if not all, of us such well-defined groups, to which we belong, are relatively few in number. But because we are all related to one another to a greater or lesser degree in such groupings, they all make some contribution to our concept of who and what we are. We live in relationship with one another, and that relationship gives meaning and purpose to our lives.[11]

A group is never static; it is dynamic, moving toward goals as a unit, and interacting within itself. A change of leaders, for example, will affect the nature and procedure (or behavior) of the group. An understanding of group dynamics makes it increasingly possible to understand, predict, and change (to improve, we dare hope) group behavior.[12]

As a professional clergyman I never had any specific training in this area of group dynamics during my formal seminary education, but I did have the good fortune to attend a Continuing Education Seminar at a midwestern theological school later on in my career, and was introduced to this aspect of religious leadership, particularly in the field of religious education. One of the texts for this course, designated as "Group Dynamics in the Church,"

was Learning Through Encounter, by Robert Arthur Dow. It is in
this book, and its fourth chapter, "The Theology For Change," that
I found the quotation used in the heading of this chapter: "God is
relationship." The Reverend Mr. Dow sees in the teachings of Jesus,
as recorded in the Gospels, the view that religion, or religions, deal
with relationships. "God is the God of relationship."[13] The statement, "God is love," (1 John 4:8) means that "God is relationship," for love (agape) is relationship.[14]

Here is an insight that spoke to me in my search for a better
understanding of God in our modern, scientifically sophisticated
world. God is known to us in terms of our relationships with the
universe and its Creator, and with one another. But there are
many kinds of relationships. Some are creative: producing new
values or new relationships. Others are destructive: destroying
those things we hold dear, and disrupting relationships. Many
relationships are neutral. They are just there, neither creating nor
destroying other relationships, but simply existing. Love, however, is a creative relationship. Out of it new relationships and
new goods (blessings) come. So God is Creative Relationship, not
only now, during this last five hundred thousandths of the age of
the universe, when human culture has developed, but from the
very first milliseconds of the Big Bang, when the universe was
born. Where is God? From the very beginning there has been
Creative Relationship bringing about order and wonder and
beauty and, yes, love out of chaos, and to me that is God at work.
But, what about destructive relationships? They are not of God,
hence they are evil, that aspect of nature and of our human existence that we have often attributed to an adversary of God, and
goodness, hence the Devil or Satan.

---

[1] Robert A. Dow, (1971) Learning Through Encounter, Judson
Press, Valley Forge, PA pp. 52ff.

Creative Relationship

[2] Cf. Genesis 1:6-8,14; 7:11; 8:2; Numbers 16:30-33; II Samuel 22:9-16; Job 9:6-9; 26:1-4; Psalms 19:4,6; 24:2; 104:2,3,5,19,20.

[3] From about 600 to 200 B.C.E., the four centuries that the Jews suffered exile in Babylonia, and returned to rebuild their nation in Palestine, codified their laws, collected their literature into a sacred scripture, and established the form of present day Judaism; the Greek philosophers developed astronomy, higher mathematics, and medicine, advanced theories of atoms and evolution, discovered the shape and size of the earth, moon and sun, and developed systems of logic and ethics. The Greek mathematician, Thales, was a contemporary of the prophets Jeremiah and Ezekiel; Pythagoras of Deutero-Isaiah and Hippocrates of Ezra-Nehemiah.

[4] A sequel, *The Valley of Horses,* by the same author, pictures what life might have been like among the Cro-Magnon who followed and displaced the Neanderthals about thirty thousand years ago.

[5] Edwin C. Krupp, (1983) "The Gods We Worship," *Echoes of Ancient Skies,* New York, Harper and Row Chapter 3, p. 63f.

[6] Ibid. p. 16.

[7] Ibid., p. 69.

[8] See Psalms 19 and 24:11.

[9] Thus, the Apostle's Creed, which actually reached its present form in Gaul in the sixth century C.E. and was adopted by the Roman Church in the eighth century, skips from the birth of Jesus, "born of the Virgin Mary," to his crucifixion, "suffered under Pontius Pilate," entirely leaving out the real meat of the "good news" he proclaimed.

[10] Malcolm S. and Hulda F. Knowles, (1959) *Introduction to Group Dynamics,* Association Press, New York pp. 15-22.

[11] Ibid., pp. 32-38.

[12] Ibid., pp. 39-62.

[13] Op. cit., p. 49.

[14] Ibid., p. 52f.

As the universe rapidly expanded and cooled in the [second] (one billionth of a second) of time, along with [forma]tion or freezing out of the four fundamental forces [described] by physics, there was a development of the fundamen[tal particl]es that go to make up the matter of our present-day un[iverse]. The first to appear, during the GUT era, 10^{-43} to 10^{-35} sec[onds,] were X-particles of a dozen different kinds: eight types of [gluons] (which hold the atomic nucleus together), three vector [bosons], and the photon.

[Du]ring the Electroweak Era, from 10^{-35} to 10^{-10} seconds, there [occurr]ed, some scientists believe, an almost instantaneous period [calle]d inflation in which the universe expanded not just at an [arithme]tic rate, as it is now doing, but exponentially. In about a [hundre]d trillionth of a jiffy, where a jiffy is 10^{-23} seconds, or the [amount] of time it takes light to travel across a proton, the universe [grew fr]om about one ten billionth the volume of that proton to [t]he size of a grapefruit. Such a rapid period of inflation, [immedi]ately preceding the Big Bang, is needed by the cosmolo-[gists to] explain the existence of clumps of matter, in the form of [clustered] galaxies, in our present-day universe. Otherwise, they [say, the] Big Bang might simply have dispersed energy uniform-[ly throu]ghout the expanding bubble of space-time, and resulted [in a fea]tureless universe in which none of us could ever be [able] to speculate about it.

[As] it was, however, at 10^{-10} seconds, the weak and electro-[magneti]c forces separated from the electroweak force, and the era [of quark]s began. By this time the universe had cooled off to some [few tr]illion degrees Kelvin, and there no longer was sufficient [energy to] create vector bosons. Quarks are the theoretical particles [that] make up present day matter, i.e., the protons, the neu-[tro]ns, and all the others that participate in the strong force [that hold]s the atomic nucleus together.[6] This helps nuclear physi-[cists e]xplain the classification of subatomic particles into octets

CHAPTER THREE

WHAT IN THE WORLD (AND UNIVERSE) IS GOD DOING?

"God is the Personal Spirit, perfectly good, who, in holy love creates, sustains and orders all."[1]

Our study, thus far, has discovered the whereabouts of God not in some far off corner of outer space, a hidden Deity little concerned with this small and insignificant planet, nor far off in times past, a First Cause in a long procession of causes and effects that proceed automatically to that maximum level of entropy where all progress stops, but rather in the creative relationships that have produced all the known universe from the naked singularity that preceded the Big Bang, and is still producing new relationships and new values today. The Big Bang, then, is science's Book of Genesis. It is the instant when space/time, the universe as we know it, was born.

Cosmologists and theoretical physicists have pushed back their hypotheses of what happened, and when it happened, to about a ten thousand dodecillionth of a second after the Big Bang. In scientific notation this is 10^{-43} seconds. It is called Planck Time named after Max Planck, the German physicist whom we considered and quoted in Chapter 1. Before this Planck Time, the energy in the still tiny, but rapidly expanding, universe was more than ten quintillion giga-electron volts, (10^{19}), where one giga-electron volt (GeV) is a billion times the energy needed to move one electron through one volt. At that time, it is believed, there was only one kind of particle and one unified force throughout the universe. Planck Time marked the instant in which the force of gravity separated from that theoretical unified force that prevailed up until that time. What the supersymmetrical universe was like prior to Planck Time (10^{-43} seconds) physicists have not yet discovered though speculations are prevalent among them. One of these is that the universe is the opposite of a black hole, in which, under the relentless force of gravity, a massive star, exhausting its nuclear fuel, collapses to an infinitely small volume of such great mass that not even light, nor any other energy, can escape from it. Astronomical evidence of such theoretical black holes has been discovered, including indications that one exists near the center of our own Milky Way Galaxy. The opposite of such a black hole, a white hole, in which there would be a great explosion of energy blasting out in all directions, is much less evident, though they are theoretically possible in quantum physics.

There may be, however, one of these white holes of which we are all aware: our universe itself. The incredibly complex reasoning that goes into such speculation, involving "event horizons", "time tunnels", and the "evaporation of black holes", cannot be set down here without the danger of writing a book within a book, but, for the curious, it can be found lucidly set forth in a book called, The Edge of Infinity, by Paul Davies, a British professor of theoretical physics.[2] Other writers on similar themes are: William Kaufmann, Harry Shipman, John Gribbin, James Trefil, Eric Chaisson, and, of course, that inimitable popularizer of science, Isaac Asimov.

At the heart of every black hole, cosmologists say, there is a singularity, which is defined as a space-time boundary, or event horizon. A terrestrial horizon is a boundary beyond which we cannot see, since light rays, or photons, do not come to our eyes

from the other side of it. So a singularity
no energy can escape from it and, hence,
tromagnetic waves, can give evidence of
cal possibility, it is a naked singularity. In
boundaries are somehow overcome so th
possibly a whole universe, can come out
ent prior causation. It has been called an
natural and supernatural" by Paul Davi
of a white hole is that it is an inside out b
say, as Genesis 1:1 does, it is the begin
began His creation.

Incidentally, modern cosmology an
port the long-held assertion of certain C
the universe was created out of nothing
so far as we have any information abou
may suppose, it was a beginning in a st
perature, density, and energy. What mi
that state our science will probably nev
known way of getting any information
a singularity, but a singularity from wh

The equivalent of a hundred mill
10^{-35} seconds, when the temperature
10^{26} degrees Kelvin, the strong force se
theoretically unified force that prevai
force is the one that binds the nucleu
separation from a grand unified force
have prevailed before Planck time, le
force still unified. This is a unificat
force and the weak force that gover
the atomic nucleus. At 10^{-10} sec
(Genesis), the weak and electromagr
are left with the four fundamental
nuclear physics.

nano
sepa
scrib
parti
verse
onds,
gluor
boson

D
occur
of rap
arithm
hundr
length
grew
about
immec
gists t
scatter
say, th
ly thro
in a fe
around

As
magne
of quar
10 quac
energy
that go
trons, p
that hol
cists to

CHAPTER THREE

WHAT IN THE WORLD (AND UNIVERSE) IS GOD DOING?

"God is the Personal Spirit, perfectly good, who, in holy love creates, sustains and orders all."[1]

Our study, thus far, has discovered the whereabouts of God not in some far off corner of outer space, a hidden Deity little concerned with this small and insignificant planet, nor far off in times past, a First Cause in a long procession of causes and effects that proceed automatically to that maximum level of entropy where all progress stops, but rather in the creative relationships that have produced all the known universe from the naked singularity that preceded the Big Bang, and is still producing new relationships and new values today. The Big Bang, then, is science's Book of Genesis. It is the instant when space/time, the universe as we know it, was born.

Cosmologists and theoretical physicists have pushed back their hypotheses of what happened, and when it happened, to about a ten thousand dodecillionth of a second after the Big Bang. In scientific notation this is 10^{-43} seconds. It is called Planck Time named after Max Planck, the German physicist whom we considered and quoted in Chapter 1. Before this Planck Time, the energy in the still tiny, but rapidly expanding, universe was more than ten quintillion giga-electron volts, (10^{19}), where one giga-electron volt (GeV) is a billion times the energy needed to move one electron through one volt. At that time, it is believed, there was only one kind of particle and one unified force throughout the universe. Planck Time marked the instant in which the force of gravity separated from that theoretical unified force that prevailed up until that time. What the supersymmetrical universe was like prior to Planck Time (10^{-43} seconds) physicists have not yet discovered though speculations are prevalent among them. One of these is that the universe is the opposite of a black hole, in which, under the relentless force of gravity, a massive star, exhausting its nuclear fuel, collapses to an infinitely small volume of such great mass that not even light, nor any other energy, can escape from it. Astronomical evidence of such theoretical black holes has been discovered, including indications that one exists near the center of our own Milky Way Galaxy. The opposite of such a black hole, a white hole, in which there would be a great explosion of energy blasting out in all directions, is much less evident, though they are theoretically possible in quantum physics.

There may be, however, one of these white holes of which we are all aware: our universe itself. The incredibly complex reasoning that goes into such speculation, involving "event horizons", "time tunnels", and the "evaporation of black holes", cannot be set down here without the danger of writing a book within a book, but, for the curious, it can be found lucidly set forth in a book called, The Edge of Infinity, by Paul Davies, a British professor of theoretical physics.[2] Other writers on similar themes are: William Kaufmann, Harry Shipman, John Gribbin, James Trefil, Eric Chaisson, and, of course, that inimitable popularizer of science, Isaac Asimov.

At the heart of every black hole, cosmologists say, there is a singularity, which is defined as a space-time boundary, or event horizon. A terrestrial horizon is a boundary beyond which we cannot see, since light rays, or photons, do not come to our eyes from the other side of it. So a singularity is also a horizon, since no energy can escape from it and, hence, no light or other electromagnetic waves, can give evidence of it unless, a mathematical possibility, it is a naked singularity. In a naked singularity the boundaries are somehow overcome so that anything, including possibly a whole universe, can come out of it without any apparent prior causation. It has been called an "interface between the natural and supernatural" by Paul Davies.[3] Another description of a white hole is that it is an inside out black hole.[4] Or, we might say, as Genesis 1:1 does, it is the beginning, when the Creator began His creation.

Incidentally, modern cosmology and quantum physics support the long-held assertion of certain Christian theologians that the universe was created out of nothing. At least it was nothing so far as we have any information about it, but in its effects, we may suppose, it was a beginning in a state of nearly infinite temperature, density, and energy. What might have existed prior to that state our science will probably never know since there is no known way of getting any information about it. It was, in short, a singularity, but a singularity from which everything came.

The equivalent of a hundred million Planck Times later, at 10^{-35} seconds, when the temperature of the universe was still 10^{26} degrees Kelvin, the strong force separated or froze out of the theoretically unified force that prevailed until then. This strong force is the one that binds the nucleus of the atom together. Its separation from a grand unified force, plus gravity,[5] which may have prevailed before Planck time, leaves only the electroweak force still unified. This is a unification of the electromagnetic force and the weak force that governs the radioactive decay of the atomic nucleus. At 10^{-10} seconds after the beginning (Genesis), the weak and electromagnetic forces separate and we are left with the four fundamental forces now recognized in nuclear physics.

Creative Relationship

As the universe rapidly expanded and cooled in the first nanosecond (one billionth of a second) of time, along with the separation or freezing out of the four fundamental forces described by physics, there was a development of the fundamental particles that go to make up the matter of our present-day universe. The first to appear, during the GUT era, 10^{-43} to 10^{-35} seconds, were X-particles of a dozen different kinds: eight types of gluons (which hold the atomic nucleus together), three vector bosons, and the photon.

During the Electroweak Era, from 10^{-35} to 10^{-10} seconds, there occurred, some scientists believe, an almost instantaneous period of rapid inflation in which the universe expanded not just at an arithmetic rate, as it is now doing, but exponentially. In about a hundred trillionth of a jiffy, where a jiffy is 10^{-23} seconds, or the length of time it takes light to travel across a proton, the universe grew from about one ten billionth the volume of that proton to about the size of a grapefruit. Such a rapid period of inflation, immediately preceding the Big Bang, is needed by the cosmologists to explain the existence of clumps of matter, in the form of scattered galaxies, in our present-day universe. Otherwise, they say, that Big Bang might simply have dispersed energy uniformly throughout the expanding bubble of space-time, and resulted in a featureless universe in which none of us could ever be around to speculate about it.

As it was, however, at 10^{-10} seconds, the weak and electromagnetic forces separated from the electroweak force, and the era of quarks began. By this time the universe had cooled off to some 10 quadrillion degrees Kelvin, and there no longer was sufficient energy to create vector bosons. Quarks are the theoretical particles that go to make up present day matter, i.e., the protons, the neutrons, pions, and all the others that participate in the strong force that holds the atomic nucleus together.[6] This helps nuclear physicists to explain the classification of subatomic particles into octets based on their properties, which is called the eightfold way, a phrase borrowed from the teachings of Gautama Buddha. Such particles are called hadrons to distinguish them from less massive leptons that do not participate in the strong force. Examples of the leptons are electrons, muons, and neutrinos.

Thereafter, though still incredibly fast by our standards, things happened at a more leisurely pace. At one microsecond (one millionth of a second) after the beginning, protons and neutrons were formed, along with their antimatter counterparts, the antiprotons and antineutrons. Most of these mutually annihilated each other, but through a fortunate circumstance the particles of matter slightly outnumbered the antiparticles, so enough were left over to become galaxies, stars, our Sun, its planets, including Earth, and us. At one ten thousandth of a second after time began, electrons formed, likewise in positive and negative forms. (The antimatter counterpart of an electron is a positron.) As these annihilated each other, radiant energy made of the universe a massive fireball, three light years across. Radiation predominated over material particles in a flash of gamma rays. But again, electrons prevailed, miraculously, in numbers to exactly match the protons.

At the three-minute mark in the age of the universe, about a quarter of the heavy particles fused to make the nuclei of helium atoms (two protons and two neutrons), releasing energy in the process. Then events really slowed down. Not until about three hundred thousand years had passed did the nuclear fireball cool down enough to permit the agitated electrons to join the nuclei and form atoms of hydrogen and helium. Thus matter assumed its more familiar atomic form for the first time. As electrons were grabbed by the protons and the combined protons and neutrons to make atoms, the electronic fog that had prevailed began to clear and the universe became transparent upon reaching its one millionth birthday. The all-pervading light of radiant energy began to fade, shifting from an intense red glow at about a million years, to an invisible infrared, and on down the scale of electromagnetic energy until now it is in the form of very cool radio waves that are only detectable with special antennas, a tell-tale signature of the Big Bang.

Since the distant galaxies are still receding at a rapid rate from our local group of galaxies due to the expansion of space-time, the superexplosion of the Big Bang, in a sense, is still going on. However, cosmologists set somewhat arbitrary limits to what they consider to be the Big Bang Era, and this usually is defined as having come to an end with the formation of atoms about three hundred thousand years after the beginning. The making of galaxies from the turbulence present in the initial phases of the universe and preserved in slight irregularities of density that lasted through that period of exponential inflation previously mentioned, began about twelve and a half billion years ago, or about one billion years after the beginning of space-time. Galaxies were formed by the hydrogen and helium atoms being pulled toward regions of greater density in the cloud of matter that had developed as the universe expanded and cooled down. In many cases densities of gas at the heart of such galaxies became so great as to form black holes at their centers, as is probably true of our own Milky Way galaxy. The massive outpourings of energy as matter is drawn into such singularities, are apparent to astronomers as sources of high electromagnetic radiation at small concentrated spots in the universe called quasars. The oldest such quasar thus far discovered is about twelve billion, two hundred million years of age. Many of them are around eleven billion years old, though undoubtedly some galaxies, and some quasars, are still in the process of formation.

Irregularities within these galaxies continued the process of matter accretion, building up stars of various sizes, and perhaps, though we have no proof of this as yet, other solar systems similar to our own.

The more massive stars have shorter life spans, using up the nuclear fuel available for fusion at a faster rate, though they may still pour forth enough energy from their nuclear furnaces for tens or hundreds of millions of years. Eventually, however, the time comes when the hydrogen that serves to fuel them has nearly all been transformed into helium. Then, cosmologists tell us, the star expands and cools, going from blue through white and yellow to red in the wavelength of light that it radiates. Still, as the outer layers of the star expand and cool, the inner helium core contracts and becomes still hotter. If the mass is great enough it may reach a hundred and forty million degrees Celsius, which is hot enough to ignite a new nuclear fusion reaction transforming helium into carbon. This means that it may continue to contract and grow still hotter until carbon fuses into oxygen, magnesium, and neon, which, in turn, undergoes still further fusion under conditions of great heat and pressure to become silicon. At the heart of such a massive star even the silicon burns, nuclearly, to make nickel and iron, which is the "end of the line" as far as the common heavy elements are concerned. When the store of such heavier atoms are exhausted as nuclear fuel, and it is no longer possible to balance the relentless contractive force of gravity with the expansive power of heat, the star collapses into a small, dense pulsar, or even denser black hole. This last spasm, however, releases a copious supply of energy, blowing the star's outer layers into space, and pelting them with high-speed neutrons which transmute some of their material into still heavier, but rarer, elements like silver, gold, lead, and many of the larger, radioactive atoms, as well.

This cloud of star-formed elements expelled from the supernova, the name astronomers give to such exploding stars when seen by them from the viewpoint of Earth, become a part of the clouds of gas and dust that float through space. And these clouds, in turn, through pressure waves produced by the supernova, may also begin to contract in spots to form new stars and solar systems seeded with the heavier elements. Our own Sun is such a second-generation star, which accounts for the fact that its four inner planets, and some of the moons and satellites of the outer planets, as well as orbiting comets and asteroids, are made up of rocks and minerals, and even, in the case of planet Earth, of the hydrocarbon compounds that could under ideal circumstances produce life.

It is undeniable that the foregoing picture of the origins of the universe, and our tiny portion of it, the planet Earth, involves a great deal of speculation. We used the word hypothesis earlier in this chapter, which may be defined as "an educated guess." Indeed, the picture of the beginning of everything that has been drawn above, is best understood as a series of interrelated hypotheses that serve to explain the myriad phenomena we detect with our senses. They are not entirely guesswork, however. For instance, subatomic particles can be briefly created in ingenious devices called linear accelerators and cyclotrons or synchrotrons, which through the controlled application of electromagnetic energy can build up energies to those approximating what must have prevailed in the early stages of the Big Bang. Furthermore, the optical and newer radio telescopes of the astronomers look out not only into distant space, but far back in time, since light requires time, even at its great velocity, to travel from one part of the vast universe to another. In fact, light or other energy from some of the more distant sources detected by our telescopes started on its way before our solar system, or perhaps even our galaxy, was formed. The hypotheses of what happened in the earliest stages of the Big Bang help to explain what the astronomers see. The point is that these hypotheses hang together and serve to bring order to our perceptions of the universe around us. What is more they bring us understanding of the processes involved in the evolution of our universe to the point where we are often able to make predictions of what new or strange phenomena we may detect when we know how and where to look for them.

Yet it bothers some among us that scientists are given so much to speculations and often to changing their hypotheses to accommodate new data, rather than in speaking with certainty and absolute authority. These people find it impressive when certain religious persons claim to be able to speak about the mysteries of who we are and where we came from with far more certainty and authority. They may even ridicule science by saying it has no way to tell what really happened in the past, since it relies for its information on observation and experimentation, and obviously there was no one around to observe or experiment back when the universe began, or even when life began. We must rely, therefore, on the only One who was there at the beginning, God, to tell us what happened, and this He has done, they say, in His revealed Word, the Bible.

As persuasive as this explanation may sound to some, the problem with it is that the claim that God has revealed all that we need to know in science and history is in itself a speculation and unfounded assumption. The nature of the Bible itself belies the belief that it is a unified whole dictated by a Divine Source to chosen persons across a few centuries of time, who acted as scribes. And its ability to offer acceptable explanations of the universe we see around us has proven, over the last two millennia, to be woefully inadequate. The Bible has its own purpose and value in the lives of human beings, along with the sacred scriptures of other peoples and cultures, to deal with questions that science does not touch upon, let alone answer, and to enhance our ability to live wisely and well with one another. But it cannot replace our learning from the book of nature, which our science teaches us how to read.

Creative Relationship

One of those who proved adept in reading that Book of nature, deciphering its language and translating it into words we understand, was an unprepossessing man, Charles Darwin, who, as a youth, had sought to study medicine, his father's profession, and, failing in that, had turned to theology with a view to becoming a Church of England priest. But his first love, as a student at Cambridge University, was the study of nature, in emulation of his naturalist grandfather, Erasmus Darwin. Soon after his graduation he was invited to become a naturalist on board the exploratory vessel, the Beagle. Though Darwin had read the evolutionary theories propounded by his grandfather, and by the French naturalist, Chevalier Jean Baptiste Lamarck, he went on that voyage with the avowed purpose of supporting, through wide observation, the essential truth of the biblical view of life's origin. The facts, as he observed them, however, including huge fossil bones of an extinct species from a dry river bed in Argentina; the savagery of the native Indians of Tierra del Fuego at the southern tip of South America and the seashells found on the heights of the Andes mountains, together with the strange species inhabiting the Galapagos Islands, caused him to question the prevailing view. As Darwin edited his notes preparatory to publishing his journal, The Voyage of the Beagle, he was forced to the conclusion that so many similar but diverse species of animals and plants could not have been separately created by "...elemental atoms suddenly transformed into living tissue."[7] He could no longer deny the obvious truth: one species gradually evolved into other species. But he did not hurry to put such conclusions into print. Over twenty long years he accumulated further data, studied the conclusions of geologists such as Charles Lyell as to the age of Earth, and the methods of selection among the breeders of domestic animals.

Early in that two decades of study he came upon an essay by Thomas Malthus on the "Principle of Population," which pictured in humanity an unrelenting struggle for survival. That thought, he quickly saw, might apply to all the world of animate nature: favorable variations would tend to be preserved; unfavorable ones, destroyed. Nature, itself, provided the selective mechanism, a natural selection.

Meanwhile, as Darwin delayed publishing his conclusions, an essay by another naturalist, Alfred R. Wallace, was sent to him for an appraisal. He was astounded at how closely Wallace's conclusions paralleled his own. How could he publish his own theory now, without being accused of plagiarism? But his scientist friends, Lyell and Hooker, proposed that both Wallace's essay, and Darwin's outline of his own view, written in 1844, should be read before the scientific Linnean Society. And so, on July 1, 1858, portions of both papers were presented to a shocked audience of scientists. Darwin was persuaded, however, to go on and publish a more detailed exposition of his conclusions, which he did in a book titled, On the Origin of Species. It was published on November 24, 1859, and the first edition of 1,250 copies was sold out the first day.

Darwin's book, of course, aroused a storm of controversy, not only in scientific circles but also among laymen and in the press. One sentence in its concluding chapter aroused most of the furor, for he had written: "Much light will be thrown on the origin of man and his history."[8] The pride of civilized, cultured man was challenged. Yet no amount of rhetoric or pseudoscience could overcome Darwin's marshalled facts and observations. Further investigations by scientists around the world only bore out the truth of Darwin's theories, and undermined all competing ones so that, today, a scientist can say, without fear of expert contradiction: "Biological evolution is not a faith. It's fact."[9]

Of course Darwin's theory has been modified and corrected over the last century and a quarter since it was presented to the scientific world, but its essential outline of a gradual evolution of one species from another, through a process of natural selection, remains firmly established. Though the laws of inheritance discovered by Gregor Mendel, an Austrian monk, had been published shortly after the publication of Darwin's Origin, they were not generally known in the scientific world, nor to Darwin himself. Mendel's research was only rediscovered at the beginning of the twentieth century. But it provided a mechanism for creating the varieties within species by mutation on which Darwin's natural selection could work. Darwin, himself, had advanced a speculative theory that changes in parental organs could be passed on to offspring through microscopic particles that he named gemmules,[10] and pictured as migrating from the various parts of the parents' bodies to their reproductive organs where they could be passed on to modify the corresponding bodily parts of their progeny. This theory he called pangenesis. Unlike his theory of natural selection, with its overwhelming supporting evidence, his theory of heredity was not widely accepted by other scientists. Mendel's investigations eventually supplied a far better one.

New discoveries in paleontology (the fossil record), however, have filled in many of the gaps in the evolutionary chain of life that Darwin had noted. Many of his missing links have since been found. But that same fossil record has shown the need for some modification of Darwin's postulation of a gradual steady evolutionary development. The effect on species of sudden catastrophic changes in climate or habitat have been documented and have led to the theory of punctuated equilibrium, or the concept of sudden spurts of evolutionary change interspersed with long periods of species stability.

This by no means undermines the overall validity of the change of species by evolution, as some religious defenders of the special creation of each species seem to think. That in large populations, well adapted to environmental conditions, individual changes would not produce much advantage and hence would be submerged in the general gene pool, is obvious. But the isolation of small numbers of certain species under marginal environmental conditions would lead to advantages for some varieties, which could then more quickly pass on their genes to the group, causing a more rapid evolutionary development. This has been found reflected in the fossil record, though, of course, most of the fossils found will be of the larger, more stable, population.

The overall picture of the evolution of life from viruses and microbes to the present millions of species of nearly every imaginable variety, has now become quite clear, even if certain details in the vast panorama of change are somewhat obscure. Planet earth was just the right size and at the right distance from a relatively small star, the Sun, so that the average temperature permitted the oxide of hydrogen, H_2O, to exist predominantly in its intermediate or liquid state and to accumulate in the depressions of the earth's crust, forming seas. Since the early predominant atmosphere of this planet consisted of hydrogen, ammonia, and methane, besides water (as is still true today for some of the larger planets of the sun's family: Jupiter, Saturn, Neptune, Uranus), the elements of carbon, hydrogen, oxygen, and nitrogen came to be dissolved in the seas to form a kind of soup of life's constituent chemicals. In the modern laboratory such a mixture, heated and exposed to some form of energy such as electricity (lightning) or radiation (sunlight), begins to produce the organic compounds found in living things. Gradually amino acids form, which in turn become proteins and nucleic acids (deoxyribonucleic acid, DNA, and ribonucleic acid, RNA) the carriers of the hereditary patterns for building organisms.

Such complex chemicals, however, by themselves, are not life. How did they become life? As yet, living things, even the most simple, have not been produced in our laboratories. How, then, did nature do it? Possibly we will never know exactly since the microscopic single cells that first appeared on earth, maybe as long ago as four billion years, left no fossil remains or traces of themselves. However, further laboratory procedures to dehydrate manufactured amino acids can produce lifelike chain molecules of complex proteins. In nature such dehydration might have taken place along ocean shorelines, or in lagoons or tidal pools. The freezing of water, too, as in polar regions, it has been found, can concentrate such acids and bases, while similar concentrations can take place in the presence of catalysts such as those found in certain types of clay.

Whether one of these, or a combination of them, actually played a part in producing the first living cell scientists may never be able to prove. But repeated energizing and dehydration under laboratory conditions have produced dense clusters of amino acids and bases called "proteinoid microspheres."[11] These protein-like compounds are dense coagulations of organic chemicals floating in a mostly inorganic fluid, and resemble bacterial cells in many ways. They possess semi-permeable membranes separating them from the inorganic medium in which they float, much like tiny oil droplets in water. These membranes permit small molecules to enter and "feed" the micro-sphere, while the discharge of wastes has also been observed. Agitation of the fluid, analogous to wave action in the ocean, has caused larger microspheres to break up into smaller ones, a primitive replication. Some of these disperse or die, but others go on feeding by absorbing molecules, and growing. Hence, while not yet true living cells, they duplicate, in a very primitive way, many of life's characteristics: eating, excreting, growing, and reproducing. Are they alive? At this level the distinction between living and non-living is not clear cut. Apparently these laboratory-produced proteinoid microspheres are somewhere in between, possibly duplicating a step by which life developed from nonlife in the early seas of planet Earth.

There is no direct evidence of a link between such chemical evolution and biological evolution. Fossils of the extremely fragile and rare early life forms can hardly be expected. Only circumstantial evidence supports the assumption that such prelife complex chemicals might eventually have achieved just the right combination of proteins and nucleic acids to become a living cell. However there is even now in our world very small and simple entities that possess attributes of both nonliving molecules and living cells. These are the viruses. All of them are much smaller than the typical modern cell. But they possess both protein and DNA, or RNA, though not much else. They lack the unattached amino acids and nucleotide bases by which living cells grow and reproduce. When in isolation, a virus is not alive. It is only a complex chemical molecule. But when it comes in contact with live cells it shows living properties. Its genes seize control and begin to dominate the cell's chemical activities. They grow and reproduce by using the cell's extra amino acids and bases, thus destroying its function, and causing diseases in the larger organisms of which such invaded cells may be a part. So, even in our present world, there are examples of non-living chemicals shading into living entities.

How or when true cells formed from the complex pre-life chemicals we do not yet know. Somewhere between three and a half to four billion years ago hungry protolife organic molecules, concentrated in shallow seas, discovered that cooperation was better than competition and combined into cells composed of protein and nucleic acid bases that could feed and reproduce more efficiently. They still fed on the "soup" of complex protein-like chemicals in the sea, but had to evolve better means of survival than that to keep from starvation when those chemicals were depleted. These first cells could copy the formation of genes and proteins occurring in the medium where they had developed, but mistakes or misprints in the gene codes due to excessive radiation or bombardment by cosmic rays caused changes or mutations. Many times such changes were fatal, but occasionally they were helpful. One of the first helpful ones was when a mutation permitted some bacteria to absorb energy from sunlight with the aid of a chemical pigment called chlorophyll that helped the cells to convert carbon dioxide (from fermentation), water and energy from sunlight into a sugar, that could feed them and set them free from dependence on the limited supply of the naturally occurring organic soup. Thus such newly energized cells flourished greatly and evolved into all the varied members of the plant kingdom, which is the basis of our food chain today.

But such cells also created opportunity for further creative relationships. Photosynthesis (the manufacture of food with the aid of sunlight) had another by-product: oxygen. This permeated the seas and spread into the atmosphere of planet Earth. Though lethal to many of the earlier fermenting cells, it opened the way for another, even more efficient, form of life.

A bit less than a billion years ago other microscopic cells evolved, through mutations, the ability to sustain themselves by combining oxygen with proteins from other living cells and thus to feed on one another. Some cells, too, played host within themselves to bacteria that specialized in using oxygen to utilize such cannibalized proteins. These guest bacteria still inhabit our cells today, and are called mitochondria. At the same time these more modern cells became better organized and arranged their genes on chromosome strings in their nuclei. From minute one-celled creatures they developed, in a relatively short time, into highly specialized organisms, some of which could swim, but others anchored themselves to underwater rocks or sand, or floated passively, becoming species which we now label as worms, jellyfish, sponges, or coral.

These species of multicelled organisms continued to evolve through sponges, coral, and jellyfish but ended in comparative

evolutionary dead ends. They produced many varieties of themselves but not much in the way of higher organisms. Worms,
however, became the ancestors of fish, chordates, vertebrates,
land animals, and humans. It would appear, then, that the prolific evangelical hymn writer, Isaac Watts, early in the eighteenth
century, was speaking more truly than he realized, when he
wrote:

> Alas! and did my Savior bleed?
> And did my Sov'reign die?
> Would He devote that sacred head
> For such a worm as I?[12]

Flatworms evolved nervous systems, hollow bodies with
internal organs, body segments, knots of nerve cells from which
brains eventually developed, eyes, teeth, backbones, gills and
flippers or limbs, lungs, scales, feathers, fur and hair, and many
of the other characteristics of animal land dwellers with which
we are most familiar. Worms became fish, some species of fish
became amphibians, some amphibians became reptiles, some
reptiles became birds and others became mammals, while the
huge reptilian dinosaurs dominated the earth. An intermediate
stage between reptiles and the placental mammals were the marsupials (opossums, kangaroos) which spread throughout North
and South America, Antarctica, and Australia when these conti-
nents were still connected with one another.

Placental mammals evolved from the marsupials about 114
million years ago, and displaced the less reproductively efficient
marsupials over most of the world's land masses, except on the
by then separated continent of Australia. Ancestors of hoofed
animals, rodents, and carnivores developed between 100 and 85
million years ago. Preprimates appeared on the evolutionary
scene about 95 million years ago, and produced the monkey-like
primates around 70 million years ago. The human ancestral
stock, evolving from the generalized mammalian form, included

tree shrews, lemurs, premonkeys, monkeys, apes (*dryopithecines*), ape-men (*australopithecines*), humans (*Homo habilis, Homo erectus, Homo sapiens*). Neanderthals and Cro-Magnons, varieties of our species, *Homo sapiens*, were the immediate predecessors of modern man. The Neanderthals appeared about 120 thousand years ago, and gradually turned into, or gave way to, Cro-Magnons around 40 thousand years ago.

We have covered vast periods of time, and relatively slow transitions in the forms of living things in only a few words; just enough to give a broad overview of the conclusions of modern biology.[13] It is also enough, however, to show how Creative Relationship, or the Power whom religious believers call God, has created our habitat, Earth, and its residents, including ourselves.

At the heading of this chapter I have given a quote from a theologian's definition of God: "God is the Personal Spirit, perfectly good, who in holy love, creates, sustains and orders all." The liberal theologian, William Newton Clark, who formulated this definition, did so on the basis of what he believed the Bible, as God's self-revelation, revealed Him to be. Dr. Clark, of course, had to carefully define what he meant, and believed the Bible meant, by such terms as "personal," "spirit," "good," "holy," "love," "creates," "sustains," and "orders." But one who reads his book, An Outline of Christian Theology, surely can have little doubt that it results in a concept with many similarities to what we call, herein, "Creative Relationship."

Creative Relationship, from a scientific viewpoint, is a process by which more complex ways of storing and using energy develop out of relatively simpler, but probably more potent in total energy content, patterns. But is this process personal, purposive, and benevolent as we believe God to be? Well, it is Creative Relationship that has, in humanity, produced personality, and it is in our relationships to others like ourselves, especially when that relationship is creative of other meaningful relationships, values, and benefits, that personhood is perceived and enhanced. God, to the theologian, is a Personal Spirit who is the origin, and therefore the original, of all persons.

That God is good is an assumption based on the belief that the creative process (i.e. Creative Relationship) has produced those relationships and substances that we hold to be of value to ourselves and hence "good." What has produced those that we call "evil" we shall leave to consider later in this book. Creative Relationship, as we have seen, is what creates, sustains, and orders all that we perceive and know.

Yet science has no way of telling whether this creative, or evolutionary process, which produced matter from energy; galaxies, stars, and planets from matter; seas and stones, plants and animals from the chemical elements and compounds that matter forms; and all the varieties and species of life, including humans, from the earliest microscopic forms that life assumed; is purposive and benevolent or not. Science deals with the what and how of the universe around us. Questions of why are outside of its purview. They are the questions that the inspired intuition in humanity, which we call religion, does deal with and speculate about. Thus science and religion, at best, do not compete, but complement each other. But since science, when true to itself, does not attempt to answer the question, "Why?" neither should religion attempt to contradict the conclusions of science as to "What?" and "How?" This is especially true because when religion attempts to do so it is generally on the basis of an earlier, more primitive, science, the conclusions of which have proved inadequate to explain newly discovered data.

But why, you might ask, have we devoted so much of our attention in this chapter to what God, or Creative Relationship, is doing at the beginnings of the universe; the beginning of matter, galaxies, stars, the Earth, life and species; and so little to what the Creator has been doing lately in human history? The answer is that too often humanity's interest has been disproportionately turned toward human history, rather than to what preceded that history. This is understandable from a biblical perspective in which human beings are created in the first week, the sixth day after the beginning. Science has quite a different perspective, of which many people are plainly unaware. In the scientific timetable of universal history, humanity did not appear on the scene until the last fifteen hundredth of one-percent of the total!

To picture it in another way: if all of the history of the universe were to be compared to a journey of 3,000 miles, about the driving distance between New York City and San Francisco, a good six-day journey for the average motorist making about 500 miles a day, then the solar system, including planet Earth, would not appear on that trip until one had traveled all across the East and Midwest and as far as the Medicine Bow mountains in Wyoming. Microscopic life would not appear on Earth until one had crossed the Continental Divide some 200 miles further on. Blue-green algae would appear around north central Nevada, and early worms, the precursors of today's vertebrates, would show up near Reno. Jawless fish would not be seen until about ten miles east of Sacramento, California, the insects in Sacramento, reptiles fifteen miles west in Davis, and modern mammals about four miles southwest of Vallejo. On this journey primates would appear near San Pablo, horses in Berkeley, apes about the middle of the San Francisco—Oakland bridge, and all of the development of humanity from ape men, through proto-men, Neanderthals, and Cro-Magnon, plus all of human history from the Stone Age to now, would lie between there and downtown San Francisco! Indeed, all the history of Christianity, from Jesus until today, would be about one and one-half feet at the end of this journey! Yet we will be paying more attention to the very short human portion of that journey in the following chapters.

¹ William Newton Clark, (1925) *An Outline of Christian Theology*, New York, p. 66.

² Paul Davies, (1980) *The Edge of Infinity*, (1981) New York. Simon and Shuster.

³ Ibid., p. 5.

⁴ John Gribbin, (1983) Spacewarps, New York, p. 50. Delacorte Press/Eleanor Friede.

⁵ Quantum physicists are still working on a definition of the force of gravity in quantum terms, and on reconciling this with Einstein's description of gravity in geometrical terms. The possibility of explaining gravity as a fundamental force involving the exchange of massless particles called "gravitons" is anticipated by many of them, but at this writing the existence of a single superforce, called supergravity, or quantum gravity, prior to Planck time, has not been established.

⁶ Quarks were whimsically named from a nonsense phrase found in James Joyce's *Finnegan's Wake*. They also come in varieties that are whimsically described: up, down, top and bottom (or Truth and Beauty), strange and charm.

⁷ Charles Darwin, (1979) *The Illustrated Origin of Species*, abridged and introduced by Richard E. Leakey, New York, p. 218a. Hill and Wang.

⁸ Ibid., p. 222b.

⁹ Eric Chaisson, (1981) *Cosmic Dawn*, Boston-Toronto, p. 185. Little Brown & Co.

¹⁰ Charles Darwin, op. cit., p. 17.

¹¹ Chaisson, op. cit., p. 164.

¹² Later hymn editors sought to soothe Christian sensibilities by making the line to read: "For sinners such as I."

¹³ More details of this magnificent history of the evolution of life can be obtained by consulting a wealth of books on the subject, such as Evolution, by Ruth Moore, for Time-Life Books in the Nature Library Series. C.f., Bibliography.

CHAPTER FOUR

"What is man, that thou art mindful of him?" Psalm 8:4a

There can be no doubt that when it comes to accounts of humanity's origin, present day biological science, and religion as proclaimed by the biblical literalists, have completely contrasting views. The Bible stories of Creation are narrated in the first two chapters of Genesis. The name of this first book in the Bible means "beginning," and it deals with the Hebrew people's concepts of the origin of things familiar in their world. These included: the starry heavens above and the earth beneath; light and darkness; water and dry land; growing plants; the Sun; the Moon; sea creatures and birds; wild beasts; domesticated cattle and the myriad "creeping things," in which they probably included snakes and other reptiles, as well as insects of all kinds. Finally were made human beings, the dominant life form on Earth, who are described as being "created in the image of God." God who, at this point, is not described or defined in holy writ, is the Creator of all these phenomena, living and nonliving, and according to Genesis He made it all in just six days, shown by the setting and rising of the sun, and "rested on the seventh day," which marked that as a significant Hebrew holy day, the Sabbath, a day to "rest from labor."

Humankind: Ascent or Fall?

There are some Bible interpreters who interpret the days, of Genesis 1 as being longer periods of time, which the Hebrew word, *yom*, like its English counterpart, could sometimes mean. This is based on Psalm 90:4, "For a thousand years in thy sight are but as yesterday when it is past, and as a watch in the night." It would help account for the fact that geology rather clearly indicates that the ages of fossils stretch out over a long period of time, involving millions or even billions of years. However, in view of the period of time involved in the age of the universe, each day would have to represent approximately two billion years! Given this problem with the literalistic interpretation, many modern Bible scholars regard the Creation stories of Genesis, as well as subsequent tales of Adam's direct descendants, the first farmer, the first murderer, the first city dweller, the first musician, the first metalworker, and the first religious believer (Enosh in Genesis 4:26); as well as the Great Flood (Genesis 6-10), and the Tower of Babel or the beginning of various languages (Genesis 11); as being mythological or metaphorical narratives. With the twelfth chapter, and the story of the Semitic ancestor, Abraham, mythology begins to shade into legend, which probably has some historical basis.

Taken literally, however, as a large group of present-day. Christians prefer to do, a pattern of human development can be presented by combining texts from various portions of the Bible. Briefly stated, this view maintains that the first man was made by God, the Creator and Supreme Sovereign of the Universe, in a single day, and in His image. Needing companionship, which was apparently not to be found in the other creatures God had made, man was operated upon by God, a rib removed and molded into woman. Then the pair, male and female, were given a select dwelling place, marked off from the rest of the barren earth, where God had planted a Garden, literally a Paradise.[1] Here was provided everything needed to keep the first humans well and happy. However, there proved to be a flaw in God's creation of these beings made in His image. They had curiosity, and a need for freedom to explore, experiment, and investigate the forbidden fruit that God had told them not to touch. They yielded to temptation and disobeyed God's commandment. The result was they were exiled from Paradise, and punished with a life of toil and pain, sweat and tears, with the Golden Age forever in the past. In short, they had fallen from grace.

Much of the rest of the Old Testament chronicles in dreary detail the sins and sadness, the trials and troubles, the strife and suffering, toward which this first failure of woman and man led. Only occasionally would an exceptional individual among humanity glimpse the possibilities of that ancient harmonious relationship with God that had been lost through humanity's disobedience and urge, in prophetic passion, a renewal of the original covenant with God. Many centuries later a new covenant was proclaimed and a new dispensation given, as a new Adam was given birth through God's Holy Spirit, a Savior who showed how the ancient Paradise had been transferred from earth to sky, and the long-standing exile could be overcome by faith in Him. As carefully set forth by St. Augustine, confirmed by John Calvin, and unanimously accepted by many branches of Protestantism, and still upheld by many of fundamentalist persuasion, Christian theology set forth the view that all humanity, being inheritors of Adam's guilt and subject to God's wrath, are damned to an eternal hell of fire. Yet God, in His infinite mercy, has chosen some human beings to be the recipients of His prevenient and irresistible grace, which saves them from their depravity and guilt, redeems them, and makes them fit for a return to the bliss of Paradise in the heavenly company of saints and angels. Through centuries of the history of Western civilization this view of the fallen nature, and unmerited redemption, of humanity has been a tremendous influence in shaping the deep thoughts of many, only coming into real question and being strongly challenged with the new doctrines brought about by scientific investigation.

The evolutionary view of the origins of the universe, the stars, Sun, Moon, Earth, life, and humanity have been set forth in considerable detail in the previous chapter. Especially in its disclosure of an alternate view of human origins and nature it presents a stark contrast to the ancient Hebrew concepts and their modern interpretation. As we have seen at the close of the previous chapter, human beings are only the most recent of a long series of changes in the forms of living things that biology labels as "evolution." Evolution is the concept that all the differing forms of life that we observe around us on earth are interrelated in that they are descendants of a common ancestor. The obvious differences in these various kinds, as the Bible calls them, or species as science now classifies them, is seen as deriving from a natural tendency among individuals of all kinds or species to vary from one another, and a process in nature whereby some of these varieties are selected to survive more readily and to pass on their changed characteristics to subsequent generations. This concept of evolution, surmised but imperfectly understood, preceded Charles Darwin and, indeed, was propounded many centuries before the time of Christ by certain Greek philosophers: Thales, Heraclitus, and Aristotle. After the "Dark Ages," in which the Christian Church had dominated the life and thought of Europe with its theological preconceptions, science, which had been kept alive by Muslim thinkers in Arabia, was reborn into the Western world, and the concept of evolution was again suggested as an explanation of the immense variety of living things on Earth, so different in many respects, and yet so obviously related in others. Jean Baptiste Lamarck, a French naturalist, proposed such an explanation in 1809, the year Darwin was born, and even added a possible theory of how it took place in the concept of "the inheritance of acquired characteristics." Before him another French scientist, Georges Louis Leclerc Buffon, had also theorized that life had evolved through natural processes. And in England, Charles Darwin's own grandfather, Erasmus Darwin, had propounded a view that evolutionary change had been brought about by the influences of environment on living organisms.

The views of Charles Darwin, whose name has been, since the mid-nineteenth century, lastingly associated with the concept of evolution, were summarized in some detail in the previous chapter. It is necessary to add, at this point, that Darwin recognized from the beginning that his book did two things: It established evolution as fact; and it proposed the theory of natural selection as to how it came about. He stated this quite clearly in his second book on the subject, dealing with human origins, The Descent of Man.

"I had two distinct objects in view; firstly, to show that species had not been separately created, and, secondly, that natural selection had been the chief agent of change... Hence if I have erred in having exaggerated its [natural selection's] power...I have at least, as I hope, done good service in aiding to overthrow the dogma of separate creations.[2]"

Certainly most modern biologists would agree that evolution is a fact, and quite as well established as any scientific fact can be. As well, for example, as the fact of gravity, and even better, perhaps, than Einstein's theory of relativity.

The first of these two propositions of Darwin was quickly accepted by scientists around the world. The second did not fare so well. Though widely accepted in English-speaking countries, England and the United States, it never received as much support in Germany and France, and none at all in Russia, where the Lamarckian views of Soviet biologist Trofim Lysenko received the Stalinist political blessing and other views were officially banned. Darwin, at least in part, developed his theory of a natural selection in the evolution of species from careful observation of the methods of the breeders of domestic animals and plants.

He even raised domestic pigeons, and came to the conclusion, after much study, that all of the various breeds, so unique in their diverse characteristics, were derived from the common English rock dove, *Columbia livia*. In considering a mechanism by which such a selection could be made in nature, as we have seen, Darwin was influenced by the reading of An Essay on the Principle of Population, by Thomas Malthus. Though primarily concerned with the problems brought on by a rapid growth in human population, Malthus had seen that the tendency to produce more offspring than can ever survive to maturity is a general principle in nature. In spite of a high reproductive capacity in most plants and animals, adult populations tended to remain relatively stable since many of the young were destroyed in one way or another before they reached a reproductive age. This essay, then, helped Darwin to grasp the important concept that there could be a selection in nature of those individuals best fitted to survive: a natural selection. Herbert Spencer, a nineteenth century philosopher, later gave this principle the label, "survival of the fittest." But, beside population pressures, as Darwin also noted, other factors entered into natural selection. In some species, nature produced variations in the male, or sometimes in the female, which were more attractive to the opposite sex. These might be size, or strength, or coloration, or display characteristics which made the individuals so gifted more likely to reproduce, and to pass on their characteristics. Also some variations made the individual members in a species more conspicuous to predators and hence less likely to survive. In human societies, as well as, to a lesser extent, among some other social animals, social pressures also played a part in the process of natural selection. Through such a process, then, science can account for both the development of the human organism, together with its mental characteristics and social relationships, and for the present-day supremacy of human beings among the life forms on Earth.

Thus evolution, both as biological "fact," and by its complex of theories as to how it came about, presents man and woman as the end-products of a long ascent from the single cell and the chemical components that make up that cell, to the complicated organisms that they are today. The picture that biological science, in the theory of evolution, presents, then, is not a "fall", but, as Jacob Bronowski labels it, in his book, and the television series based on the book, an *Ascent of Man*.

Discoveries of fossils in the primate family tree are still being made, quite frequently in fact, especially in Africa. This means that the details are still somewhat in a state of modification and subject to change, but the overall picture of humanity's ascent is fairly clear. Early in the history of mammalian evolution, some-where around 185 million years ago, there existed, according to fossil evidence, a small quadruped, about the size of a rat, but more resembling a shrew, that paleontologists call a *mega-zostrodon*. These creatures were probably egg laying, like the present-day duck-billed platypus, but were undoubtedly mam-mals. The dinosaurs still flourished at that time and mammals did not advance much, but did well simply to hold their own as an inconspicuous minority against the reptile competition. When the dinosaurs died off at the end of the Mesozoic Era, about 65 million years ago, leaving only a few reptile survivors such as birds, crocodiles, lizards, turtles, and snakes, mammals were enabled to come into their own and began to multiply greatly in both numbers and varieties. From the shrewlike mammal men-tioned above, the ancestors of the modern tree shrews undoubt-edly developed, and also the ancestors of the prosimians, such as the tarsiers and lemurs. From these, in turn, evolved the mon-keys of many varieties. According to fossil evidence found in the once lush, but now very desertlike Fayum Depression, some 60 miles southwest of Cairo, Egypt, there lived around 35 million years ago a higher primate, ancestral to present-day apes, and humans, *Aegyptopithecus*. This cat-sized primate was a tree-dwelling fruit eater and, unlike its descendants, possessed a tail. It had a brain size of about 30 cubic centimeters, which in conjunction with its small size, made it probably the smartest animal of the Oligocene epoch, from 38 to 26 million years ago. In time, it appears its descendants came down from the trees.

How human beings gradually evolved from these earliest animals on the primate family tree is a story that has unfolded largely in reverse. Modern humans have only been on the European scene for the last 45,000 years, about seven times the length of historic times. Though their fossil remains, called Cro-Magnon, were first discovered about a dozen decades ago in the Vezere River Valley of south central France, about 70 miles east of Bordeaux, it is now plain that they were widespread on every continent except Antarctica. Artifacts and fossil bones of this type of human have been found not only in great numbers throughout Europe, but also in the Near and Far East, Australia, Africa, and North and South America. These show that such human beings were very skilled in making stone and bone tools and weapons; that they were remarkably gifted artists; that they used and kindled fires and were good hunters who cooked the meat of the animals they killed. Probably, also, they had highly developed language skills and communicated well. Though they lived and buried their dead in caves in limestone rock in central France, so their fossil remains were best preserved there, they no doubt used other types of shelters in other places and also adapted their clothing to the type of climate in which they lived.

Like modern humans they probably had varying superficial characteristics, such as skin, hair and eye color, and differing cultural practices in the various places where they lived. Also the times varied in which they discovered and used various technologies.

However, their brains were quite uniform in size, averaging around 1590 cubic centimeters in volume, somewhat larger than the present-day average of 1330 cubic centimetres. Where did these modern humans, designated scientifically and perhaps somewhat presumptively, *Homo sapiens sapiens*, come from and how are they related to other human types or varieties that have been discovered? One of these types that preceded Cro-Magnon, going back some 75,000 years earlier to 120,000 years ago, was Neanderthal Man, *Homo sapiens neanderthalis*, first found as a fossilized skull cap, ribs, pelvis and limb bones in a small cave in the Neander River valley near Dusseldorf, Germany. This was in 1856, three years before the publication of Darwin's Origin, fifteen years before his book on human evolution, The Descent of Man, and twelve years before the discovery of the Cro-Magnon remains in France. Actually fossils of the Neanderthal type were found in Europe as early as the 18th century, but were not recognized as belonging to a distinct human species. Since then they have been found and properly classified in many areas throughout Eurasia and Africa. It appears, however, that Neanderthals did not spread into Australia or the Americas. Fossils of more than a hundred of them have been uncovered over widely separated sites in Europe, Asia, and Africa. Neanderthals were shorter but probably heavier than most modern humans are. Their bone structure was more massive, and they were strong. Their brains were, on the average, larger than those of present-day humans but their heads and faces, were, from our viewpoint, misshapen. Their heads were long, and comparatively flat, with foreheads sloping toward the back. Their faces protruded and jaws receded more than ours do. There were pronounced brow ridges over their eyes and larger cheekbones than we have. This was especially true of the European Neanderthal specimens that have been found, and this may give us a somewhat exaggerated picture of what they looked like, since Europe is where most of the discoveries of Neanderthal fossils have been made. In addition one of the earliest more complete Neanderthal skeletons to have been studied seems to have been that of a man who was arthritic, or, perhaps, had rickets, and this tended to give a distorted concept of what he looked like. Subsequent comparisons of Neanderthal fossils from around the Old World indicate that they probably varied as much in appearance as we do.

However that may be, it is plain, from accompanying artifacts in their cave habitations, that they made quite sophisticated stone tools and weapons, fashioned charms or amulets, used pigments to decorate themselves, flowers and roots as folk remedies for illnesses, buried their dead in honor and respect, and decorated their graves with flowers. They were skilled hunters who sought game animals such as the woolly mammoths, wild horses, reindeer, and bison, as well as smaller animals such as foxes and wolves. Marks of spirituality and ceremony are also indicated in the skulls and other bones of the giant cave bears they preserved and arranged in shrines, and the evidence that they cared for the elderly, sick, and handicapped individuals among them.

Yet the image of their brutish appearance, as portrayed in the early literature about them, has led many, laymen and scientists alike, to feel that they cannot have been the direct ancestors of modern humans, and this may be right. Other skulls nearly twice as old as the Neanderthal ones have been found at Swanscombe on the Thames near London, and at Steinheim in France and Bilzingsleben in Germany. These are sufficiently modern looking to have secured a classification as archaic *Homo sapiens*. Then, still before Neanderthal times, from about 128,000 years ago, comes evidence that such archaic humans ate large quantities of shellfish at the southern tip of Africa. Still earlier archaic *Homo sapiens*, called Rhodesian Men, and possibly ancestors of an African variety of Neanderthal, lived in what is now Zimbabwe. Other examples of this archaic type have been found in Tanzania. This indicates that two different species of Homosapiens may very well have shared the world between them during this long period of time, and that the modern *Homo sapiens sapiens* may be descendants of the one that was more modern looking than the Neanderthals. Still, someone may ask, what evidence do we have that either one of these might have been ancestors to *Homo sapiens sapiens* and the people of our time?

We identify ourselves, in the present, by our family name, a mark of our ancestry, at least in the patriarchal line, and by the lands from which our ancestors came. In my own case both of my parents came from Warwickshire, England, and, aside from a few cousins in Canada, most of my relatives now live there. My mother was born into a family of eleven siblings, besides her father and mother, and the family name was Winnett. An uncle in Canada, James Winnett, who made a study of his genealogy, found that back in the eighteenth century the family name had been Gwinnett, but that somewhere along the line they had later dropped the initial G. One of the more adventurous young men in the family back then had traveled to the New World where he made his way somewhat obscurely in the colony of Georgia until the revolt against the Mother Country that began in 1775. Then allying himself with the colonist's cause, he was chosen to represent his adopted homeland as a delegate to the Second Continental Congress of 1775—76, which produced the Declaration of Independence. He was one of its signers. His given name was Button.

On a trip to Great Britain in 1977 to visit some of my relatives that we had never seen before, my wife and I had the good fortune to be given a copy of my Grandfather Taylor's marriage record from 1868, which showed his name to be Edward, and that at the age of twenty-one he had married an Eliza Edwards. Her father, and hence one of my great grandparents, was Richard Edwards, while my great grandfather on the Taylor side turned out to be Robert Taylor.

Humankind: Ascent or Fall?

This is as far as I have ventured to go back in tracing my ancestry but I know that besides the above named ones I had two more grandparents, and six more great grandparents. Going back another generation I would have had sixteen great, great grandparents, and the generation before that thirty-two direct ancestors, and the one before that, sixty-four, and so on. One more generation back would be two centuries before our present one, and more than a hundred direct ancestors of mine would be living then. Back a thousand years there would be over a billion of them. But the entire population of the world was only about 280 million then, proving that second, third, and fourth cousins have often been marrying without realizing their kinship. Even dividing that figure by 1,000 to compensate for such overlapping of ancestors, I would still have had over a million individual direct ancestors back at the time the Vikings were invading much of Europe, including England, and exploring even as far west as the mainland of North America. Probably some of these Norsemen would be numbered among my ancestors.

Two thousand years ago, around the time of Christ, even dividing by a billion for overlapping when the world population was much smaller, I still would have had over a billion ancestors which would have included all of the people in the world thousands of times over. Not all of them could have been my ancestors, however, for the peoples of the Orient, the Aborigines in Australia, the Indians in North and South America, for example, were too isolated to have intermarried with ancestors of mine. However, these might well have included all the Romans, who controlled the Mediterranean politically at that time, and all the Greeks who gave that Classical World its culture. No doubt many might have been Semites, Phoenician traders, who plied the ports of the known world with their ships, or Jews, who had been dispersed throughout the Roman Empire. There might even have been some Egyptians or black Ethiopians among them. But the bulk of them would have been Germanic, Gothic, or Celtic tribes-men of Europe, primitive hunters or agriculturists, by any mod-ern standard, savages. Go back to forty thousand years ago and surely every one of the Cro-Magnons then spreading throughout Europe would have been an ancestor of mine, with probably a mixture of similar humans from other areas, since *Homo sapiens sapiens* were great travelers. It is quite possible that some of them mated, somewhere, with Neanderthals. There are fossils that were found on Mount Carmel in Palestine that look like they might have been a cross between Cro-Magnon and Neanderthal.

This likely genealogy for me is almost duplicated for you, whoever you are; though there may be some differences along the line in racial characteristics and ethnic balances. The point is that we all share an almost identical gene pool, since we are all, basically, brothers and sisters. This is true whether we look at the biblical view of our origins, or at the conclusions of biological sci-ence. The Bible would make us even more closely related, since our one common ancestor, Adam, would have lived only about 6,000 years ago! Even as prolific as some of the biblical patriarchs were reputed to be, it is hard to see how there would be six bil-lion people presently in the world in that short a time, however. The more believable view is the biologist's one that our common ancestor lived about thirty-three times that long ago, about 200,000 years before the present, in Africa.

This conclusion was derived from genetic studies of a wide variety of racial groups on Earth at present. Since the discovery of the nature of genetic material in 1953 by biochemists Francis Harry Compton Crick and James Dewey Watson, using a tech-nique developed by physicist Maurice H. F. Wilkins, a triumph for which all three were awarded a Nobel Prize in 1962, it has been possible to date biological changes by changes in the molec-ular structure of DNA in the cells. Assuming a fairly constant rate of molecular change, an assumption that has been borne out by studies in various biological lines, it has been concluded, for example, that chimpanzees and humans shared a common ancestor only about five million years ago. Prior to this most paleontologists had believed that the separate human lineage went back two to three times that far.

The genetic structure of a human being is far too complex to draw any conclusions concerning the whole molecular pattern of a human individual, but it so happens that in each of our cells there is what seems to be the genetic material of a bacteria that was incorporated into eukaryotic cells about a billion years ago. These are the mitochondria, which enable such cells to make use of the oxygen in the atmosphere for the metabolizing of food. The mitochondria are only passed on to new generations through the female line, from mother to daughter to granddaughter, and so on. This is because the cellular part of our inheritance comes only from our mothers. The sperm cells contributed by the father, though they have mitochondria, too, only pass on their nuclear genetic material of DNA and RNA to the ovum at conception. Males too, of course, have mitochondria, inherited from their mothers, in all their cells, including the reproductive ones, but they cannot pass them on to their children. Since the genetic structure in mitochondria is much simpler than in the whole human organism, it is easier for the biochemist to trace genetic changes in it. So studying the changes that have taken place in the genes of the mitochondria have enabled geneticists Rebecca Cann and Allan Wilson to arrive at the conclusion that the common great grandmother of all humans alive today lived about 200,000 years ago, probably in south central Africa![3] Presumably our ancestry traces back to the male who fathered her daughters, as well, though his genetic contribution is now untraceable. The human species who lived at that time, according to the fossil evidence, was either Archaic *Homo sapiens*, who was then coming to the end of his approximately 300,000 span of years on Earth, or, perhaps, his successor, *Homo sapiens*

sapiens who in that isolated center of the African continent may have just been coming on to the scene as an evolutionary modification in this line. Possibly this ancient grandmother of all humanity was a transition between what we now consider to be two different hominid species, a missing link now discovered.[4]

Archaic *Homo sapiens*, like his cousin, *Homo neanderthalis*, probably evolved from an earlier hominid now known as *Homo erectus*. What was this ancestral hominid species to modern humanity like? Considerable fossil evidence of their physical makeup, as well as their characteristic activities, has been found since a skull, teeth, and thigh bones were discovered by a Dutch army physician, Eugene Dubois, on the island of Java in 1890. Four years earlier, a famous German naturalist, Ernst Haeckel, on the basis of his study of Darwin's writings, predicted that such a missing link would soon be found and gave it the scientific designation, *Pithecanthropus erectus*, meaning erect ape-man. Scientists since then, sure that it represents an early human species, rather than a manlike ape, have renamed it *Homo erectus* or erect man. Seven years later a jaw bone attributed to the same species was found near Heidelberg, Germany, but not until twenty more years had passed was another one, called Peking Man, found in western China. The more intensive searches of the twentieth century, however, have turned up the fossilized bones of about a hundred individuals of the *Homo erectus* species, and these have been found widely scattered throughout Indonesia, China, Africa, the Middle East, and Europe, indicating that this early human was a widely traveled hunter. The oldest fossils of *Homo erectus* have been found in the Olduvai Gorge in East Africa leading scientists to speculate that they spread out from this original homeland and traveled as far as their bipedal locomotion could take them. In one and a quarter million years, of course, that was quite far. The Chinese caves where their bones were found indicated that they used fire, while remains of their habitations in France and hunting expeditions in Spain indicate that they lived in huts, used cooking pots, probably made of wood; fished, and hunted big game by using fire to drive animals. Their tools and weapons were exceedingly primitive as compared with those of the Cro-Magnons, or even the Neanderthals. They consisted mainly of stone hand axes, or rough stone blades for cutting up the animals they killed in hunting. No spear or arrowheads were found. If they used spears, as they probably did, these most likely were of wood with points perhaps hardened in a fire. Still they were a very successful species as indicated in the length of time they survived on earth, probably as the master predator of their age. This is one thing that we have surely inherited from them, since in the two hundred millennia that modern man has been on Earth, he has quite evidently been responsible for the extinction of many other species.

Tracing *Homo erectus* back to his probable African origins, it is quite clearly indicated that he evolved from an even more primitive species that is still classified by modern biology as human. This is one whose fossil remains and artifacts have been uncovered in Olduvai, Tanzania, by the famous Leakey family of paleontologists. Among the fossil remains of Australopithecines, or southern apes, which are quite prevalent in various African locations, the Leakeys found evidence of a creature that closely resembled the *Australopithecus africanus*, but which had half again as large a brain volume, about 750 cubic centimeters, and one that evidently made and used stone tools quite habitually. They named this new discovery, *Homo habilis*, or handyman. This earliest species of Homo or man, lived for nearly as long a span of time as his successor, *Homo erectus*, during a time when several species of hominids roamed the African veldt. Living about that same time were the larger ape-men species, *Australopithecus robustus*, and *Australopithecus boisei*, as well as the slighter variety of southern ape, who evolved into *Homo habilis*. In short there may have been three or even four species of hominids engaged in the struggle for survival in Africa at that period of time, but of them all handyman no doubt was the smartest and best equipped to survive because of his brain and tool-making skills. We don't know that he had any language beyond a few grunts and warning cries, and perhaps some signs by which he could communicate commands or responses. Neither is there any evidence that he could use his stone tools as hunting weapons to any large extent. They seem to have been crudely sharpened stones for chopping or cutting, though he might have been skillful at throwing them to bring down small animals. Otherwise he may have survived mostly by driving away other scavengers or predators to steal their prey. The southern apes in their turn seem to have evolved from a smaller, less brainy, but still erect-walking predecessor which is called *Australopithecus afarensis*, the fossils of which were first found in the Afar triangle of Ethiopia by anthropologist Donald Johanson and his associate, Thomas Gray, in 1974. This was the famous woman whom they named "Lucy" after the Beatles' song, "Lucy in the Sky with Diamonds," which was very popular at that time. Lucy was only about three and a half feet tall and weighed approximately fifty pounds. She walked erect, but her brain size was only about 450 cubic centimeters, a little less than that of a modern chimpanzee. However, she lived about three million years ago, and other members of her species later discovered in Ethiopia go back as far as 3.7 million years. This antedates the *A. africanus*, which was larger and had a larger brain. And it begins to approach the five million years ago separation point that the geneticists give for the common ancestor of chimps and humans. Ancestral to these may have been the *Dryopithecines*, who are believed to be forerunners of modern apes, and perhaps of the human lineage, too. One of the earlier specimens of these, Proconsul, was so named because it was believed to be an ancestor of Consul, a chimpanzee living in the London Zoo in the

1930s, and, indeed, it seems possible that this ape ancestor, who lived around ten million years ago, might have been that descendant of *aegyptopithecus*, that led eventually to the ape and the human lineage.

Our human ancestry, then, traced back some ten million years or so, reveals a remarkably rapid ascent from a monkeylike creature with a comparatively small brain, to the "naked ape" of the present with a brain that is huge in comparison to its body size, and a culture and technology to match. There are animals, such as the whale and the elephant with larger brains, but they also have much larger bodies for that brain to control, and hence seem to have no portion of it left to develop a comparable technology or culture. It seems evident to the scientists that what gave human development such an advantage was the acquiring of an erect stance, using only two legs for walking, and having two limbs free to develop into very versatile manipulative devices, the arms and hands. This took place when the ancestral southern ape, of which the famous Lucy was one, learned to walk more habitually erect than the other apes, though she and her kind evidently still spent a lot of their time in the trees. This was not all, of course. She, like other primates, developed a close social relationship with others of her species. They formed family or tribal groups in which they shared the food that was obtained, and mutually protected one another.

Curiosity in these early hominid creatures, unlike the case of the biblical Adam and Eve, led to something good in the investigation and manipulation of their environment, which in turn helped to develop their brains still further. The *australopithecines* themselves, or their immediate successors, the handymen, learned a new technology in the making of stone tools, and then, in erect men, stone weapons to make them more efficient competitors with the larger predators. Each such advance gave more impetus to further investigation and understanding of their relationship to the world in which they lived, and hence more control over it. They improved their fashioning of stone implements. They learned how to make use of plants and herbs for garnishing their food and providing home remedies for their ills. In time, as modern humans came on the scene, they learned to use art to inform, to inspire, and lift the spirit.

Their brains had fashioned a language of sounds to better communicate ideas, and they learned to make signs and pictures to represent such ideas, and to leave a record for posterity. This led, in time, to writing, and then to history, and then to the development and communication of abstractions. The ability to perceive relationships led to mathematics, the symbolic language of relationships, while learning mathematical manipulation led to concepts of logic and constructive thinking which have so greatly contributed to the development of modern science.

Advances in just the last six generations, or two hundred years, have enabled us to slip the bonds of this, our home planet, and send men to walk on the Moon; to fly through the air faster than a bird; to travel over the ground faster than any other animal can run, or over the water, or under it, further than any fish can swim; to harvest the resources of the earth for our benefit; to multiply greatly our food sources for sustaining life, and the remedies, natural or manmade, that will cure our ills; even, finally, and most characteristically human, to bring into significant relationship the forms, colors, and texture of wood or stone and pigment to create great art; to create great and not so great literature; and even to capture on the chemical coating of film or magnetic tape the episodic or changing scenes of our daily life. We supplement our brains for both memory and for thought processes with computers, such as that small terminal on which these words are now being written. Indeed, it is beyond our ability even to list, and keep current in our encyclopedias, the continuing triumphs of our technology. By any measure of ability to grasp and use our relationship with the world around us, and control our life for good, or evil, we have surely ascended from our lowly animal origins, and more closely approached what humans have always considered to be the abilities of their gods.

"To control our life for good or evil," we say. But what do these religious, or philosophical, terms mean? What is good and what is evil? What is right and what is wrong? To speak in specifically religious terms, what is sin and what is righteousness?

As the noted psychiatrist, Karl Meninger, asked in his notable book on the topic of morality and ethics, "Whatever Became of Sin?" His answer was that by and large modern Western civilization simply changed the label on it. What was called sin in the older Christian religious tradition has been more recently called: crime, a symptom of some mental aberration, a mistake, error, transgression, infraction, or maybe even "an outgrown concept." With the growth of the modern nation, and the development of a comprehensive and complex legal system, many former sins of the Church have become crimes through legislation enacted by our lawmaking bodies. Legal penalties, rather than spiritual ones, have been attached to the commission of such socially undesirable deeds. This has narrowed the concept of sin, which used to include the evil thought as well as the evil deed. Most attempts to attach legal proscriptions to thoughts as well as actions generally result in overly oppressive societies and ultimate social failure.

But what is sin? In the Judeo-Christian tradition it is defined either as disobedience to the law of God as this is set forth in the revelation of the Holy Writings, or a failure to measure up to the ideal standard as demonstrated in the life of Jesus the Christ. The Hebrew words, *chet*, or *chata* (chattath) and the Greek *hamartano* or *hamartaria*, commonly translated "sin" and "to sin" have essentially the same meaning. However, the emphasis is frequently quite different. For example, compare passages on this subject from Leviticus 6:2-7 with Romans 3:21-25a:

If anyone sins, and commits a breach of faith against the Lord by deceiving his neighbor or through robbery, or if he has oppressed his neighbor, or lied, swearing falsely—in any and all the things which men do and sin therein, he shall (make restitution), and the priest shall make atonement for him before the Lord, and he shall be forgiven for any of the things which one may do and thereby become guilty.

But now the righteousness of God has been manifested apart from the law, although the law and the prophets bear witness to it, the righteousness of God through faith in Jesus Christ for all who believe. For there is no distinction; since all have sinned and fall short of the glory of God, they are justified by his grace as a gift, through the redemption which is in Christ Jesus, whom God put forward as an expiation by his blood, to be received by faith.

These two passages, one from the Old Testament, and the other from the New Testament, are illustrative of this different emphasis. Righteousness or sinlessness, in the Old Testament, is usually, though not exclusively, based on strict adherence to an ethical or moral code. In the New Testament, on the other hand, righteousness is commonly based on a relationship to God through Jesus Christ. In both the Old and New Testaments, the verbal forms, *chata* in Hebrew, or *hamartano* in Greek, could be literally translated, "to miss the mark." But in the Old Testament the mark that is missed is the legal standard set up in the laws attributed to Moses, while in the New Testament it is the "measure of the stature of the fullness of Christ."

In either case sin is best understood as a breakdown in relationships between the believer and his or her God. The remedy for it is to find some means of restoring that relationship: in the older Israelite covenant by sacrifice, obedience, and forgiveness; and in the newer Christian covenant by trust in Christ as Savior, forgiveness through Him, and a new effort to measure up to the standard He sets. This accords well with the concept of God set forth in these pages: God as Creative Relationship. Evil, as we have previously defined it, is Destructive Relationship, while neutral relationships, which are neither creative nor destructive, may neither disrupt nor enhance our fellowship with other persons, including our God, but, given too much priority and attention in our lives, they may impede our achieving of that Creative Relationship that will make us at one with our God. In that sense these neutral relationships, too, may become sins.

We may leave it to other literary sources, including the Bible itself, of course, to give detailed lists of sins and their consequences. In this volume, which takes an overall theological perspective, we cannot be soporifically exhaustive in going into details. Suffice it to say that it is sin which disrupts good, value-producing relationships, and the way to avoid it, or correct it, is to restore creative relationships, or seek that Creative Relationship which is God.

The sages, prophets, and teachers who have shown humanity how to do this have been many throughout history. We might mention Moses, and the 8th to 6th century BC Hebrew prophets, Buddha in India, Confucius and Lao Tzu in China, Socrates and Plato in Greece, Jesus of Nazareth, Epictetus in Rome, and Mohammed in Arabia. And there were the students or followers of all of these who either explained, or sometimes altered, their teachings. To most of us in the occidental world, of course, it is Jesus, whom we call "the Christ," who was the prophet and teacher par excellence. And it is to His life and teachings we turn in the next chapter.

---

[1] The Greek, paradeisos, literally "enclosure," was used in the Septuagint, the Greek translation of the Old Testament to render

the Hebrew , gan, "garden."

[2] Charles Darwin, (1863) The Descent of Man, London, John Murray.

[3] Reported in the Reader's Digest, Vol. 131, No. 785, September 1987, p. 94, and in a NOVA Program, "Children of Eve," presented over Public TV in 1987.

[4] An earlier estimate, based on a previous study, gave the date of this maternal ancestor of modern man as about 600,000 years.

CHAPTER FIVE

THE WORD MADE FLESH!

(Jesus of Nazareth)

"And the Word became flesh and dwelt among us full of grace and truth; we have beheld his Glory, glory as of the only Son from the Father."   John 1:14

Jesus was a man, a historical personage. This is an assertion that has been frequently challenged over the last two millennia. Christian theologians have set forth the proposition that he was and is a unique God/man, a merging, in some miraculous way, of the divine and human natures. Laypeople of this faith, possibly even a vast majority of them, have not infrequently believed that he is more God than man, though this is a conclusion that several of the New Testament writers did their best to repudiate. The clergy, who presumably have studied these biblical writings with some care, as well as the writings of the theologians of their faith, have often not tried hard to disabuse the laypersons of this notion, and perhaps have sometimes even encouraged it.

On the other hand some historians have gone to the extreme of denying that Jesus even existed. They have sought to show how teachings and miraculous deeds attributed to Him were current in the literature and traditions of His time, and how a group of rebels against the somewhat rigid doctrines of Judaism might have made Him up to promote their own views.

To discover any firm facts about the real Jesus of Nazareth from the welter of conflicting opinions about him is a daunting task. Even the four gospels of the New Testament, which are virtually our only source material on the life of Jesus, are far more propaganda documents, designed to win adherents to the Christian faith, than they are historical or biographical writings. Those who wrote them were men of faith, already convinced that this man, Jesus, was the culmination and challenger of, as well as the ultimate authority over, human history and not just another figure in it. In reading their portrayal of him as Messiah and Son of God, as well as teacher, lawgiver, prophet, priest, and king, we face a monumental task in sorting out the human Jesus from the idealized portraits of him. We have equal difficulty in sifting out the actual words of Jesus from the multitude of words about him.

However, legendary accretions and imaginative idealizations are a part of the biographies of nearly every ancient figure of great acclaim. This applies to political persons of note as well as to religious ones; for example, to Alexander the Great, Julius Caesar, and Genghis Khan as well as to Confucius, Gautama Buddha, Mohammed, and Moses. We don't question their existence because of the exaggerations found in their biographical information. Neither need we do so in the case of Jesus of Nazareth.

To be sure authentic historical references to Jesus in ancient sources outside of the New Testament are meager indeed. An incidental one comes from the Roman historian, Tacitus, c. 115 AD, who in explaining the blame being put upon the Christians for the disastrous Roman fire of 64 AD and their subsequent persecution, refers to the derivation of their name as coming from one, "Christus", who was condemned to death for insurrection by Pontius Pilate, the Roman procurator of Judea, during the reign of Tiberius. Another is found in the history, Jewish Antiquities, written by Flavius Josephus, c. 37-110 AD, who refers to the trial and death by stoning of "James, the brother of Jesus, who is called Christ."[1]

In these and other historical sources, there are longer and more laudatory references made to Jesus called "the Christ," but these are suspected of being later additions made when Christianity was a much more widespread and powerful force in the Greco-Roman world. In its beginnings the religion that looked to Jesus as its founder was one that caused authorities some problems in local areas but had very little impact on the affairs of the far-flung Roman Empire as a whole. The religion that within three centuries began to have a major influence on all the subsequent history of Western culture, like its founder, had humble beginnings.

The traditions preserved in the Gospels concerning Jesus' birth and childhood are moving and well-loved stories even among people who are otherwise little touched by Christian teachings and concerns. However, they are also largely legendary or, one might say, even mythical in character.[2]

For example it is generally assumed that Jesus was born in Bethlehem in Judea, about 5 miles southwest of Jerusalem. And yet, the Gospel of Matthew, with which the New Testament begins, makes clear this site was selected as his birthplace because of a prophecy, recorded in the Old Testament Book of Micah, that an ideal king of the royal line of David would again come from that small village, which was David's birthplace. And so, by tradition, it was believed that the Messiah or "anointed one," (in N.T. times translated as "the Christ") would also come from there. Still Matthew's Gospel and that of Luke, which agrees that this was the birthplace of Jesus, have some contradictory and somewhat farfetched explanations of how it came about that Jesus, later recognized as having been a native of Nazareth in Galilee, was born, instead, in Bethlehem.

In Matthew, Joseph and Mary have a home in Bethlehem in

which their baby, Jesus, was presumably born. But then astrologers from the east, probably Zoroastrians from Persia, come looking for the child whose birth star they have seen in the heavens. They arrive in Jerusalem and inquire about the birthplace of the new "King of the Jews." Old King Herod who has ruled there for more than thirty-five years, and is jealous of any possible successors, even among his own sons, is greatly concerned as to when and where this royal birth may have taken place. He makes inquiries of his chief priests and experts in the scriptures as to where it might be, and they, on the basis of the prophecy found in Micah, tell him that it must be in Bethlehem. He directs the astrologers there, but then sends his soldiers to follow them and massacre all the children under two years of age (indicating that the Magi had told him that this birth might have been as much as two years earlier). Joseph, having been forewarned in a dream that the massacre is coming, flees into Egypt with his family and remains there until Herod dies. Then, because he hears that Herod's son, Archelaus, is ruling in Judea in Herod's stead, he migrates to Nazareth in Galilee. What the story doesn't take into account is that another son of Herod, Antipas, was reigning in Galilee, and he, as it turned out was the more dangerous of the two.

The Gospel of Luke, on the other hand, has Joseph and Mary living originally in Nazareth of Galilee, and because of a census decreed by the Roman Emperor Augustus, they have to travel to Bethlehem, the home of Joseph's ancestor, David, to be registered. There the time of Jesus' birth arrives, and they have to find accommodations in a stable (or at least some place, possibly the courtyard of the inn, which has a manger). After receiving a visit from shepherds, who heard angels announce the birth out in the fields where they were taking care of their sheep, Joseph and Mary remain in Bethlehem a little over a week, and fulfill the Old Testament requirements by taking their firstborn son to the

Temple in Jerusalem to offer the required sacrifices for his redemption. Then they return home to Nazareth, with no time for a visit to Egypt even though Matthew had cited a prophecy (Hosea 11:1) that God's Son would come out of Egypt. Such discrepancies and the tying of the Nativity stories to supposed Old Testament predictions concerning the coming of an ideal future king, lead many scholars to suspect that the accounts of Jesus' birth are legendary in nature.

Furthermore the date of Jesus' birth is left in as much doubt as its locale. It is well known, of course, that a Russian Monk, Dionysius Exiguus, living in Rome in the sixth century of the Christian era, was the one who calculated that this significant event occurred in the year 753 AUC on the Roman calendar. That was a mistake, for by that date King Herod, who figures prominently in Matthew's account, had already been dead for four years! Faced with this miscalculation for the beginning of anno domini, "the year of the Lord," historians have had to conclude that Jesus may have been born four or five, or maybe even six or seven years "BC" (i.e., before Christ).

The evangelist Luke's dating of the marvelous event doesn't help much, either. As noted above, he ties it up with a census ordered by Augustus Caesar for the "whole [Roman] world," which, he says, was carried out in Palestine by Rome's Syrian legate, Publius Sulpicius Quirinius. This, we are told, involved an order that each head of a household had to return to his ancestral home city to be registered for taxing. This is given as the reason that Joseph, being of "the house and lineage of David," had to undertake the 80- to 90-mile journey on foot or, perhaps, as traditionally, with a donkey for his pregnant bride, to Bethlehem, where Jesus was born. Now Quirinius, according to the meticulous records of the Roman bureaucracy, was legate (or governor) in Syria for three different terms: 6-4 BC, 3-2 BC, and 6-9 AD. It is known that Augustus started making such census enrollments in

23 BC, and every fourteen years thereafter, in provinces under Roman control. One would have been due, therefore, in territory under Syrian supervision around 9 BC. Some theorize it might have taken a year or so to get the job completed, so it might have been during Quirinius's first term, around 6 BC. On the other hand, King Herod, a friend of Rome, was then the absolute monarch in power in Judea, and it is unlikely the Romans would have ordered and carried out a census in his territory under the supervision of the Syrian governor, even aside from the obvious logistical problems that would have arisen in the masses of Palestinian residents having to leave their jobs and take to the highways to go back to the places from which their ancestors came. On the other hand we know that there was a Roman census in Judea in 6 AD, for it caused a revolt, reported by Josephus in his history as being led by a certain "Judas of Galilee."[3] The Romans quickly suppressed it and Judas was executed. This, however, was in 6 AD, and it is hardly likely that the birth of Jesus took place at this late date. It is quite possible that Luke was confused about his dates (749 or 759 AUC) and that there was no connection whatever between a Roman census and Jesus' birth.

We may surmise, then, that Jesus, who is not infrequently designated as being "from Nazareth" or a "Nazarene" in all four Gospels and the Book of Acts, was born in that Galilean village and of human parentage. The Gospel According to John reports that people identified him as "Jesus of Nazareth, the son of Joseph," and offers no rebuttal to that identification. And Matthew and Luke, in spite of their espousal of the tradition of his virgin birth to Mary, carefully trace his ancestry back to Abraham (or even to Adam in the case of Luke) through Joseph. The problem is that they disagree on the name of Joseph's father and many other names in Jesus' ancestry, and even on the number of generations between King David and his descendant, Jesus. Furthermore they disagree on which of David's sons,

Solomon or Nathan, was the one through whom that descent took place. Obviously the attempt was being made, in spite of the stories of Jesus' miraculous birth without benefit of a human father, to show that he had the proper ancestry to fulfill the Old Testament prophecies concerning the Messiah.

In either case, however, this was inconsistent with the contention that Jesus fulfilled a "prophecy" found in Isaiah 7:14 that the future Messiah would be born to a "virgin". Reading the context of that verse in the seventh chapter of Isaiah shows us plainly that it was a sign to be given to King Ahaz of Judea more than seven centuries before Jesus was born. A baby son was to be born to a young woman, perhaps the prophet's own wife, and his name would be Immanuel ("God is with us") to signify to Ahaz that he should trust God that his enemies would not prevail over him. It was unfortunate for subsequent Christian theology that the translators of the Septuagint, the Greek version of the Old Testament, used a Greek word, *parthenos,* meaning, specifically, "virgin," to translate the Hebrew *almah* which meant "mature" or "of marriageable age" whether married or not. If the prophet had meant "virgin" he would probably have used the word *bethulah* which meant "separated", hence a virgin.

That Jesus was a descendant of David, however, is not unlikely in the light of what we noted in the previous chapter concerning the proliferation of ancestors for any individual over a period of many generations. This was even more likely in the case of David, who had at least half a dozen wives, and Solomon, who is reputed to have had seven hundred wives and three hundred concubines! Nearly every Jew in Palestine, by the first century of the Christian era, could probably have traced their ancestry back to David in one way or another.

On a more scientific level, the ancestry of Jesus was similar to ours, as a descendant of the *Homo sapiens sapiens* species and the hominids preceding it. Once again the evolutionary lineage outlined in the previous chapter as being our heritage as humans also applied to Jesus, as it did to Abraham, Moses, Alexander the Great, the Roman Caesars, Mohammed, Confucius, and Buddha. Jesus left no direct descendants, according to the biblical record, but no doubt we are somewhat indirectly related to his ancestors, as he was related in one way or another to King Herod, Pontius Pilate, and Judas Iscariot.

Mark, the first Gospel in respect to its date of composition, omits the more legendary traditions concerning Jesus' birth and ancestry, and begins its story of his mission and message with his fateful decision to leave his father's trade of carpentry and launch upon a prophetic ministry. This is connected to the preaching and symbolic actions of his predecessor, John "the Baptizer."

That this colorful wilderness preacher was indeed a figure of some prominence about this time in Palestinian history is supported by the testimony of Josephus, the previously mentioned Jewish historian of the last half of the first century of the Common Era. Indeed he receives a much longer and more detailed citation in Josephus's Jewish Antiquities than Jesus does. The passage cites Herod Antipas's execution of "John, who was called the Baptist," because he was fearful "that the great influence John had over the people might put it into his power and inclination to raise a rebellion..."[4]

The four Gospels and the Book of Acts make plain that, prior to his execution, the fiery evangelist, John, had been a popular figure in Palestine, and had acquired quite a following of disciples, though there is also apparent, in these writings, a conscious attempt to downgrade the predecessor, John, and promote his successor, Jesus. It does seem likely, as the New Testament record affirms, that Jesus went to the banks of the Jordan where John was preaching and accepted baptism at his hands. The earliest Gospel, Mark, states this in bold and unequivocal fashion.

Later Gospels, however, apparently were not pleased with this recognition of John's primacy in time and its implication of priority in authority. In Matthew's Gospel John is made to protest Jesus' request for baptism saying, "I need to be baptized by you. Why do you come to me?" And Jesus graciously permits him to do it by replying, "It is fitting for us to do this to fulfill all righteousness." Luke carries this subordination of John a step further by reporting, in his Nativity story, that John's mother, named Elizabeth, was a relative of Mary, the mother of Jesus, and that when Mary went to visit her during the time when both women were pregnant with their divinely ordained children, John shifted in his mother's womb in greeting to Jesus, leading to Elizabeth's exclamation of a blessing which has become a part of the Roman Catholic Church's honoring of Mary. In addition Luke barely mentions the baptism of Jesus, while the fourth Gospel, John, omits it entirely! It is obvious that if the Gospel writers had any inkling that the baptism of Jesus by John was not a historical fact they would have been happy to leave it out of their accounts.

We can be fairly sure, therefore, that the impetus for the beginning of Jesus' short career as an itinerant preacher and teacher in Galilee, and subsequently, but briefly, in Jerusalem, was the mission of John the Baptizer to be a "voice in the wilderness," in the tradition of the Old Testament prophet, Elijah, calling for repentance in Israel and a return to the righteousness commanded by God, and baptizing people in the Jordan River as a sign and symbol of that repentance.

Neither the Gospels, which omit mention of them, nor Josephus, who does give much information on the Jewish sect called the Essenes, connects John to that group whose nature and teachings have been brought to light in the discovery of their scrolls and the artifacts of their community at Qumran in the Judean wilderness near the Dead Sea. However, the geographical juxtaposition of the traditional site of John's activity with that community plus the similarities of his reported message to that of the Essenes, suggests that he had some connections with it. There is, however, no evidence either in the Gospels or elsewhere that Jesus did.

The first three, or Synoptic[5], Gospels indicate that following Jesus' baptism, he faced a crisis in determining the course of his mission. This is in the form of apocryphal stories about his being tempted (or tested) by Satan. Mark's rather brief and comparatively restrained reporting of this period of contemplation or pondering by Jesus on how to conduct his God-given task is elaborated by both Matthew and Luke into a series of three temptations which could only come to a kind of Godlike figure. Jesus was alone when all this took place for he had not yet acquired any disciples. And it would seem quite unlike him to have later imparted to them any personal details of what influenced his decision to become their leader.

All four gospels agree that Jesus recruited a group of about a dozen followers or trainees called disciples, to learn his religious viewpoint and, later, to be sent out two by two to take it to various communities, most likely all in Galilee. Whether purposely or not, the reported number of disciples, twelve, corresponded to the number of the tribes of Israel in Old Testament times to signify, perhaps, that this was a message for all of Israel. There are some minor disagreements in lists of these followers between Luke in his Gospel and the Book of Acts, and Mark and Matthew in their Gospels. Generally, these are viewed by scholars as alternate or surnames for those listed. Only a half dozen are much more than mentioned, except in John's Gospel which goes into more details about such obscure figures as Philip, Nathaniel (Bartholomew), and Thomas.

A brief, but instructive, summary of Jesus' early mission in Galilee is given by Matthew in Chapter 4, verses 23 to 25, just prior to his three chapter summary of Jesus' preaching or teaching that is known as The Sermon on the Mount. It reads:

> He went throughout all Galilee, teaching in their synagogues and proclaiming the good news of the kingdom. He also healed every sort of disease and illness so his fame spread into all of Syria and they brought to him those who had various diseases and severe pains: the demon possessed and mentally ill, as well as the paralyzed, and he healed them. Then large crowds came to him from Galilee and the Ten Towns, from Jerusalem and Judea, and from Transjordan.

This passage tells us that his primary message was an announcement of the coming reign of God, and that he attracted large crowds to hear him by curing people's diseases, handicaps, and pains. It is interesting to note that the illnesses named in this summary are all maladies that might be psychosomatic in nature, at least some of the time. In a time in human history when medical science was still very primitive and dependent, in large part, on spells and incantations for the relief of the sick, such a combination of authoritative teaching and miraculous acts of healing was expected. That the mind of the sick person is very influential in the course of any disease even modern physicians will tell you and faith in their skill and in the medicines they dispense are still very necessary to any successful cure.

John Romer, in his highly informative book on the Bible and history, Testament,[6] points out that the Pool of Bethzatha in Jerusalem, close to the Sheep Gate, where John's Gospel (5:1-18) tells us that Jesus healed a paralyzed man, has been discovered by archaeologists to have been built on the site of an ancient shrine to Aesculepius, the Greek god of healing. That is why, in Jesus' day, the rectangular pool was surrounded on four sides by colonnades or porches with roofs supported by pillars, with a fifth colonnade built across the center, so that it could, as John says, have "five sto'as" (or porticoes). It was a gathering place for sick or handicapped people seeking to get into the pool when the water was roiled and be cured. The archaeologists also found under the rubble some votive tablets given by people in recognition of the cures they had experienced. In this it was much like other shrines, both ancient and modern, such as Lourdes in France, where crutches, bandages, and inscriptions, giving testimony of those who were cured of their ills, are to be found.

This is not to say, however, that every miraculous cure reported in the Gospels as being dispensed by Jesus, including the cleansing of lepers and the raising of dead persons, actually took place. Reports of even minor cures are often exaggerated in the retelling, and many of the Gospel accounts bear clear evidence of some other purpose than a mere record of Jesus' prowess as a healer. They sought to establish plainly his special relationship to God, and the authority of his message. The force of his personality and the compelling power of his conviction, no doubt, could have convinced many that he had miraculous powers to heal. But always in such cases there is a tendency in the retelling of these stories to exaggerate the marvelous nature of the cures. This tendency can be seen reflected in the Gospels themselves as you move from one Gospel to another and compare their retelling of the same event. It is even more pronounced when you move from the Synoptic Gospels to a reading of the Gospel According to John, where the healings are signs of Jesus' divine nature and God-given power and less a matter of his compassionate reaction to human suffering.

One case in point is the central miracle in John, Chapter 11, of the raising of Lazarus from his tomb after he had been dead for four days. It is indeed puzzling to the casual reader of the Gospels to find that this startling and convincing demonstration of the divine power of Jesus is not so much as mentioned by the other Gospel writers. In fact Luke, who does tell us about Mary and Martha of Bethany, and records a pleasant vignette about their entertaining of Jesus in their home, does not even mention that they had a brother named Lazarus. This is inexplicable if Luke knew the story about Lazarus being raised from death. On the other hand, at about the same juncture in Jesus' brief career where John puts the story of the raising of Lazarus, i.e., shortly before the final week leading to the Crucifixion, Luke has a parable about a beggar named Lazarus who died and was carried by angels to a blessed afterlife in Abraham's bosom. The rich man at whose gate Lazarus had lain, suffering from hunger and sores during his lifetime, also died and suffered the torments of Hades. Looking up from his suffering and seeing Abraham far off he cried out, "Father Abraham have mercy and send Lazarus to dip the end of his finger in water and cool my tongue, for I am in anguish in this flame." But Abraham replied, "Son, remember that in your lifetime you enjoyed all the good things while Lazarus suffered evil. Now there is a great chasm over which he cannot pass to you, nor you to us." So the tormented rich man begged that Lazarus might return from the dead to warn his five brothers and save them from coming to such a place of torment. But Abraham responded, "They have had Moses and the prophets to tell them, and if they do not listen to them, they will not be convinced by someone rising from the dead, either." It is significant that the lesson of the parable in Luke (16:19-31) is the same as that of the miracle in John (11).

While admitting, then, that the Gospels are accurate in claiming that Jesus attracted crowds of the curious by seemingly miraculous cures as well as by the freshness and implied authority of his teachings, we should still be cautious about taking any one, let alone all, of the reported miraculous cures as "the gospel truth."

It is by the quality and originality of those teachings, of course, and not in the miraculous signs, which, in spite of certain charlatan claimants among his present-day followers, are unrepeatable, that Jesus still speaks to humanity today near the close of the twentieth century. We shall consider those teachings in more detail in a later chapter, but here let it suffice to say that they were presentations of thoughts and doctrines that challenged both the religious and social preconceptions of his day, and set forth a way of life based on the perception and establishment of right relationships between ourselves, our fellow human beings, and our God.

As a further example let us consider the kind of attitude and response recommended by Jesus for dealing with opponents or enemies. Nothing is more natural in our present-day world, even as it was in the ancient world, for one person to resent, and to respond in kind, to another who by word or conduct indicates opposition or hatred. Thus it often is in the relationships between nations in our world, even the nations that happen to dwell in Jesus' homeland, Palestine, and its surrounding areas. Such a reaction is commonplace even among groups of Christians. Note, for example, the three centuries of warfare between Protestant and Roman Catholic extremists in Northern Ireland, or, closer to home, the battles, mostly in words fortunately between fundamentalists or modernists in the various Christian denominations. Why is it that among Jesus' self-proclaimed disciples of today there is so little heed paid to his words recorded by both of the Gospels according to Matthew and according to Luke:

I say to all who hear me, continue to love your enemies and to treat well those who hate you, to bless those who curse you, and to pray for those who abuse you. To those who in anger slap you on one cheek, turn the other cheek also, and from the one who takes your coat, do not withhold your shirt. Always give to anyone who begs from you, and from those who steal from you don't demand it back. Do to others as you would like them to do to you. If you only love those who love you back, what credit is that to you? Even the heathen love those who love them. And if you only do good to those who do the same to you, what credit is that to you? Even the heathen do that much. Or if you only lend to those from whom you hope to get something back, what credit is that to you? Even the heathen will lend to one another when they expect to get equal value back. So love your enemies, and do good, and lend expecting nothing in return and your reward will be great for you will be children of the Most High who Himself is kind to the ungrateful and the wicked. You be as compassionate as your loving Father is.[7]

Most non-Christians of today would consider that counsel of how to conduct human relationships to be stupid, and even most Christians probably regard it as highly impractical. So, few, if any, people in our world are willing to try it. In our system of laws, as well as in our daily affairs, most of us think it is smarter to follow the way of retaliation. Pay others back as good as you get. Do to them as they do to you. Seek to destroy your enemies, and to get back at those who hurt you. In the relationships between Jews and Arabs, between communists and capitalists, between whites and blacks, rich and poor, that is the code of conduct you will most often find. But the way that Jesus taught is the way of creative relationships as he saw it revealed in God who is Creative Relationship (love).

What gave the teachings of Jesus such originality, force, and authority was the consistency of his actions with what he said. He lived by his code of creative relationships. This molded his conduct toward other people, but even more than that, it expressed the depth of his relationship with the God of his fathers, whom he felt comfortable in addressing as "Abba, Father." The Gospels reveal that he included in his love and concern (i.e., his extended family with whom he lived creatively) not only good friends and companions, like the twelve followers whom he had chosen, but women who were second-class citizens in that society, the "common people who heard him gladly," some of the Pharisees who were open to him and sought to learn from him, (e.g., Nicodemus, who, however, is mentioned only in John's gospel) and some of the wealthy class who found him interesting (e.g., Joseph of Arimathea).

To be sure this did not keep him from being critical of those, especially the ones claiming to be superlatively religious, who did not demonstrate such creativity in their relationships. This included many of the Pharisees who were extremely judgmental of the religious quality in the lives of the common, ordinary people, and the Sadducees, the party of wealth and power, who often treated others as persons to be exploited for their own gain. This means that while there were many in Galilee whom he had helped and inspired and who loved him, there were others in positions of power and influence who feared and apparently hated him. Where Jesus, a man of a different culture and background, still has immeasurable influence on the world of today is in the evidence of the early Christian testimony that he went to a painful and ignominious death for refusing to compromise his principles.

The largest portion of the record in all four gospels deals with the circumstances of Jesus' death and the events leading to it. Approximately one third, or five out of Mark's fifteen chapters, deals with one week between Palm Sunday and the dawn of Easter morning. About 26 percent of Matthew and 19 percent of Luke cover the same period of time. John's Gospel, which has much discursive material, raises that percentage to about thirty-eight. It may well be presumed that the events of that trying week remained fresh in the minds of the Apostles and was the subject matter of much of their discourse to others over the years until the Gospel records were finally written.

Mark's account of this final week in Jesus' earthly life is arranged into a day-by-day account, and for the most part Matthew and Luke here, as they do throughout, accept his outline.

On the first day of the week, Sunday, Jesus participates in a tri-umphal parade into the Temple City of Jerusalem, the arrange-ments for which have apparently been previously made, thus indi-cating it was a planned event. Conscious, no doubt, of an oracle of Zechariah (9:9), which Matthew cites, Jesus had made arrange-ments to borrow a donkey's colt on which to ride into the city. Some of the Galilean pilgrims to the Holy City for the Passover observance, recognizing Jesus and his disciples, spread their gar-ments on the road ahead of him, and others took branches from the field which they spread on the road, or waved as they shouted,

God save us. Blessed be the one who is coming in the name of the Lord. And blessed be the coming kingdom of our father, David. God save us completely.

Understandably the Pharisees were disturbed by this demonstration, which might be interpreted by the Roman gover-nor and his legions as an incipient revolt. According to Luke's account they even called to Jesus to silence his followers, but he responded, "If these keep silent, the stones will cry out."

According to Mark, after entering the city Jesus went to the Temple and looked around, but since it was getting late in the day he returned to Bethany with his twelve disciples. Matthew, apparently on the theory that on first seeing what was going on in the Temple courtyard Jesus wouldn't be able to permit it to continue a moment longer, puts the dramatic act of the driving out of the merchants and moneychangers on that first day, but Mark postpones the event until his return on Monday.

The next day, Tuesday (Monday by Matthew's reckoning), was a day of disputation and argument, first with the chief priests, scribes, and elders over his authority for doing what he had done, then with the Pharisees and some of the supporters of Herod Antipas who tried to trap him into making some state-ment that would make a charge of subversion stick. Following his escape from that entrapment, along came some of the Sadducees who wanted to argue with him about the resurrection in which the Pharisees believed but they did not. Finally, after pronouncing a series of woes on the Pharisees for their hypocritical behavior, Jesus had a chance to sit down in the courtyard of Temple and watch the comings and goings of the people. He called his disciples' attention to a poor widow who out of her poverty put into the offering boxes all that she had and contrasted her gift and its acceptance by God with those of the rich people who ostentatiously made their contributions. This leads to a special section called "The Little Apocalypse" which is partly a prediction of the destruction coming upon Jerusalem in the near future, and partly a promise of the eventual coming of the Messiah (or a return of Jesus as the Son of Man.) This is most likely an addition supplied by the Gospel writers or the early church from another (possibly written) source.[8]

It would seem that this might have been enough to occupy a couple of days, but Mark implies that on Wednesday, while Jesus remained in Bethany dining in the home of Simon the (cured?) Leper, his enemies were in Jerusalem plotting their strategy to arrest and kill him.

Then, on Thursday, the first day of the feast of Unleavened Bread, he sent his disciples to prepare an early Passover meal in Jerusalem (possibly in the home of Mark and his mother, Mary), which became the Last Supper, followed by the vigil in the Garden of Gethsemane, and Jesus' arrest and preliminary trial.

Lengthy studies have been made of Jesus' two trials, one before the Jewish Council, the Sanhedrin, administered by the chief priest, and the other before the representative of the Roman Empire, Pontius Pilate. However, these can be summed up by the observation that it was a hastily contrived and unorthodox proceeding designed by the Jewish leaders to get Jesus out of the way before the highly sacred occasion of the Passover observance should begin. In the first, held late on Thursday night or early Friday morning, Jesus was charged with blasphemy on the testimony of some hired witnesses, and then tricked into making an admission of his views that technically substantiated that charge, for which the punishment was death. However, being unable to carry out the death sentence themselves, the chief priest and his minions arranged to have Jesus turned over to the Roman Governor, Pilate, with a different charge, that Jesus was a revolutionary who sought to make himself king. According to the Gospel record, at least, Pilate seems to have seen through this unsubstantiated charge, and tried to find some way of releasing Jesus, but was finally dissuaded from that by the demonstrations of an aroused and unruly mob. He took the course of least resistance, and condemned Jesus to death on a cross, a form of capital punishment reserved for the most desperate and despised criminals.

The four Gospels all draw to a close with a climax of tragedy, the carrying out of that sentence, and the death of Jesus on the cross. One can sense the deep despair of his disciples and friends, not to mention the members of his family who had tried to dissuade him from such a challenge to the religious and political authorities. Luke expresses it well in the comments of a couple of his disciples to their risen leader whom they failed at first to recognize. As they walked along toward the village of Emmaus about five miles west of Jerusalem, they encountered a stranger, who asked them what they were talking about with such sad countenances.

"Can you be the only one in the area who doesn't know what happened in Jerusalem?" asked one named Cleopas.

"What happened?" the stranger asked.

They explained,

Concerning Jesus, the Nazarene: He was a prophet powerful in deed and word in the presence of God and all the people. But the chief priests and rulers turned him over to be sentenced to death by crucifixion. He was one whom we had hoped was to deliver Israel. (Luke 24:17-24)

Yet, as this and other stories in Matthew, Luke, and John indicate,[9] there was a further, more stupendous, climax, a renewal of hope and of faith in the victory of Jesus over death. Partly this was due, as indicated both in the Gospels, and in the letters of Paul of Tarsus, whose correspondence constitutes so much of the New Testament, to visionary experiences of Jesus alive again, and apparently more powerful and authoritative than ever. Also it was due to immediate reports that women followers, and some of his disciples, had visited the tomb outside the city wall and found it empty. These reports, affirmed by three of the Gospels, may yet be suspect since Paul, who is at pains to set forth the evidence for Jesus' resurrection (I Corinthians 15), fails to mention them. But, if they are true, we are left with the question of what happened to the body of Jesus? To that question we shall return shortly, but first let us ask in what sense, if any, we may accept the New Testament and subsequent Christian assertion that Jesus was divine.

Some five centuries before Jesus walked the dusty roads of Galilee, a Greek philosopher named Heraclitus lived about 500 miles to the northeast of Palestine at Ephesus in Asia Minor. As did other Greek philosophers of the fifth and sixth centuries, Heraclitus speculated on the basic stuff of the universe, that which was the fundamental reality of which all the great variety of things were but manifestations. Thales, who was later considered to be the founder of Greek science, mathematics and philosophy, had thought that this basic reality was water. Anaximander, a pupil of Thales, thought it was a kind of intangible, ether-like substance that pervaded the universe. Anaximenes, a pupil of Anaximander, opted for air as the basis of all matter. Xenophanes who began to teach philosophy a few years later opined that it was earth, while Heraclitus believed it was fire, which had the obvious power to change things and was so ever-changing itself.

This seems to be, and was, wild speculation, for the great Greek thinkers of the time were not given to experimentation, which is the way modern scientists test theories. Heraclitus, however, while he viewed the world around him to be in a state of constant flux, or change, felt that there must be something back of it all that was unchanging, stable and permanent in a changing world. To that unchanging reality he gave the label logos, which basically meant "word," but could also mean "reason" or "intelligible structure." By extension it could also mean "knowledge." This is the sense in which it has come down to us in the labeling of many branches of modern science: e.g., archaeology, knowledge of ancient things; biology, knowledge of life; geology, knowledge of the earth and, of course, theology, knowledge of God.

In spite of a lack of system or structure, and of experimental testing of their hypotheses, the various Greek philosophers came up with some remarkable anticipations of the conclusions of present day science. Thales, for example, accurately predicted an eclipse of the Sun for May 28, 585 B.C.E. His pupil, Anaximander, recognized that the heavens revolved around the Pole Star, and deduced that this meant that they were spherical in nature. He also thought that all life originated in water, with which conclusion modern biologists agree. Anaximenes was the first to maintain that the rainbow was a natural phenomenon rather than a goddess. Xenophanes maintained that since fossil seashells were frequently found high in the mountains, these must have been once covered by the sea, and by some stupendous force been raised to their present height. Though also affirmed by James Hutton, the founder of modern geology, in the 18th century, the process by which it takes place has only recently been investigated by the scientific study of tectonics. In the same way, the postulation by Heraclitus of a creative, intelligible reality, which he called "logos" or "word," has recently been given more substance by the science of communication and its development of information theory.

Information theory is primarily an outgrowth of the scientific investigations of two different men during World War II. The first, from the point of view of seniority, was Norbert Wiener, a mathematician. He was born in Columbia, Missouri, on November 26, 1894. He was a child prodigy who entered Tufts University at the age of eleven, and earned a doctorate from Harvard in mathematics before his nineteenth birthday. Later he studied under Bertrand Russell at Cambridge University in England and then under David Hilbert at the University of Gottingen in Germany. Later still he became a noted professor of mathematics in his own right at the Massachusetts Institute of Technology. While he was at M.I.T., World War II broke out and soon scientists from that institution and Bell Laboratories were called in to help work out problems of tracking enemy bombers and V-1 "buzz bombs" over England and thereby to improve the accuracy of antiaircraft guns. They were successful in building automatic electronic devices which, with the help of the newly invented radar, could track a flying target, compute its position, direction, and speed, and predict where it would be by the time a shell traveled from the antiaircraft gun to the target area. This American-designed device went into service on the east coast of England in August 1944 and so improved the accuracy of the guns that whereas they had previously shot down only 10 percent of the V-1 bombs, they could thereafter destroy 50 percent of them. Through this work Wiener became interested in working out the mathematical basis involved in the communication of information and using it to control mechanisms. In 1948 he published his conclusions in a book titled, Cybernetics. This branch of science dealt with the fundamental mathematical relationships governing such automatic controls.

The Word Made Flesh!

Claude Elwood Shannon was the other mathematician who was instrumental in the development of Information Theory. He was born in Petoskey, Michigan, on April 30, 1916, and pursued his undergraduate studies at the University of Michigan. He went on to earn a Ph.D. in mathematics at M.I.T., where one of his professors was Norbert Wiener. Then he joined the staff of the Bell Telephone Laboratories in 1941. There he became involved in the problems of more efficiently transmitting information. In wartime he worked on secret codes that also touched on this problem of transmitting information. Eventually Shannon worked out a method for expressing information in mathematical terms. This he did on the basis of the Boolean algebra that was formulated by the nineteenth century mathematician, George Boole, which can be expressed in terms of the binary number system that is also used in computers because any number can then be expressed in combinations of on/off switches in the computer circuitry. Shannon's work made the computers useful for more than rapid calculations of mathematical problems. It made them instruments for the processing of information. Also his work related information to Ludwig Boltzmann's mathematical formula for entropy in the second law of thermodynamics: $S = k \log W$, where S stands for entropy, k is a universal constant known as Boltzmann's constant and W is the number of ways in which parts of a system can be arranged. Shannon determined that the mathematical expression for a quantitative amount of information bears a striking resemblance to the above formula for entropy, which Boltzmann had ordered to be carved on his tombstone. The logical conclusion is that information and energy are closely related, even as Wiener had once been quoted as saying, "Information is entropy." Modern information theory suggests that nature must be interpreted not as matter and energy alone, but as matter, energy and information.[10]

As the work of Wiener and Shannon has been followed up by

further investigations, it has been determined that information theory has applications in many different fields of human knowledge. This is not surprising since knowledge is information. David Layzer, a Harvard astronomer, has applied it to a theory of the cosmos, i.e., to the whole universe, in explanation of why the universe seems to be running down in energy with increasing entropy but simultaneously seems to be increasing in complexity and order through the generation of more and more information.[11] Sir Arthur Eddington's metaphorical arrow of time is split into two arrows, one of entropy and one of history. They are not contradictory but complementary according to Shannon's theory of information. Both follow logically from what happened in the Big Bang.[12]

Information theory is also seen, in Jeremy Campbell's book, to apply to such diverse realms of science as genetics, biological evolution, theories of perception, and the structure of the human brain, and through these to the bases of art and music, of languages and mathematics, and even basic reality, the T.O.E. or theory of everything. The quanta into whose mysteries we delved in the first chapter, turn out to be nature's means of communication. We so use them in our radios and television sets. The energy waves, which make up the electrons, protons, neutrons, as well as the subtler particles of matter such as the quarks, the neutrinos, the cosmic rays and alpha particles, and the theoretical gravitons which impart the force of gravity, may all be seen as various means of imparting information from one part of the universe to another. The universe is made up of matter, energy and information, and without the information to bring order out of chaos, there would have been plenty of energy, but never any matter, and no knowledge of the universe in which we live.

This, then, makes the *logos*, or word, conceived by Heraclitus some five centuries before Christ, a basic reality in the universe propounded by modern science, and makes more meaningful than he could possibly have known the statement by the author

118

of the Fourth Gospel that: "The Word became a human being and lived among us."[13]

Jesus, as Incarnate Word, may be seen as God or Creative Relationship communicating with that triumph of the long process of evolution, a self-conscious, reasoning being, Homo sapiens sapiens. A careful examination of Jesus' teachings, as preserved in the early Christian literature, which will be undertaken in a subsequent chapter, shows him to have been a matchless exponent of the workings of Creative Relationship in human affairs.

It also makes far less mystical hyperbole the evaluation made by the Apostle Paul of Jesus as a divine figure in his Letter to the Colossians, Chapter 1, verses 15 through 20, which in a free translation reads:

He [Jesus] is the image of the invisible God, the firstborn of all creation, for by him everything else was created, both on earth and throughout the universe, both that which can be seen and that which is unseen, even all kings and ruling authorities, all were created by him and for him. So he is over all, and all things are held together by him. He is also head of his earthly body, the church. He is its founder and the first to be raised from the dead so he is supreme over all things. For God was pleased to completely dwell in him, thus reconciling everything to himself on earth or in the whole cosmos, bringing all the universe into right relationship to himself through the blood shed on his cross.

So, it would seem, Jesus was sensitive to and perceptive of the nature of God as Creative Relationship to the degree that he was able to impart his insight to his followers and through them to the wider world of humanity. They came to see God in him, not just in his teachings, but in the way he lived and died, and thus came to the natural conclusion that he was divine.

This, however, is not the same thing as saying he is God. That was a subsequent development as the story and message of Jesus as a Jewish Messiah (Greek, Christos) was taken out into the Greco-Roman world. Controversies over the nature of Jesus Christ led to the development of an orthodox Christology which looked upon him as an earthly manifestation of God and eventually to the concept of the Trinity: one God in three Persons. Jesus probably would have been as puzzled as many later Christians have been over who and what the later theologians said he was.

We see the beginnings of this development reflected in some of the Letters of Paul of Tarsus and in the Fourth Gospel. While the Synoptic Gospel writers are quite circumspect about equating Jesus with God, the Gospel according to John and the Johannine Epistles, as well as the Epistles of Peter, and, as we have seen, some of the Pauline Letters go quite far in making or implying that identification. Some of this was due, no doubt, in Christianity's coming into contact with the Greek culture where the concept of a human-shaped deity was not at all uncommon. As careful as the early Christian leaders were in trying to keep out the influence of pagan ideas on Christianity, Gentile believers almost unconsciously and automatically kept bringing them in. And this was particularly true in respect to the preaching of the Resurrection as the basic Gospel message.

----

[1] Flavius Josephus, *Jewish Antiquities*, XX, 9, 1, quoted in Bornkam, op. cit., p. 28.

[2] Definitions of "legend" and "myth" are given in Chapter 5A.

[3] Morton S. Enslin, (1938) *Christian Beginnings*, New York: Harper & Row, p. 68.

[4] Flavius Josephus, XVIII, 5; cited in Enslin, (1938) Christian Beginnings, New York, p. 150. Harper and Row.

[5] Matthew, Mark, and Luke are called Synoptic Gospels because a connected summary or synopsis can be made of their

contents. It seems that both Matthew and Luke depended on Mark for the outline of their Gospels. This is not true of the Fourth Gospel (John), which has a different outline, and substantially different material. The Gospel According to John should be considered as a dissertation, or even a drama, portraying the writer's insight into the nature of Christ. It probably cannot be relied upon for accurate biographical or historical material.

[6] John Romer, (1988) Testament, New York, Henry Holt and Co. pp. 161ff.

[7] Luke 6:27-36, c.f., Mathew 5:39-42; 44-48.

[8] Note the parenthetic comment in Mark 13:14 (Matthew 24:15)"let the reader understand."

[9] Mark's gospel ends abruptly with the discovery of the empty tomb, but has various endings in the manuscripts, supplied, evidently, by those who felt it had ended without telling the whole story.

[10] Jeremy Campbell, (1982) *Grammatical Man*, New York, Ch.1, pp.12,16.

[11] Ibid., p.p.84-86.

[12] C.f., Chapter 3.

[13] John 1:14a.

CHAPTER FIVE
APPENDIX

WHAT HAPPENED TO THE BODY OF JESUS?

"Behold, I tell you a mystery..." I Cor. 15:51a

Each of the four Gospels in the New Testament end in chapters that propound a mystery—what happened to the body of Jesus? There is no consistent answer to that question, however, since each one tells a somewhat different story. Dovetailing them together which, as we have seen, is what the average casual reader generally does with varying Scriptural accounts we get the following story.

The second day after the Crucifixion, due to an intervening Sabbath, one or more of the women who had followed Jesus, and who, unlike his disciples, were present at the foot of the cross, decided to visit the tomb where his body had been laid. According to some of the accounts, their purpose was to anoint the body with fragrant ointments and spices, as orthodox burial custom required. In the Fourth Gospel, however, this was not really necessary since two friends of Jesus, Nicodemus and Joseph of Arimathea, had supervised the entombment and the wrapping of the body in a shroud impregnated with about a hundred pounds of a myrrh and aloe mixture. The import of the telling of this story, in other words, is not to give their reason for the visit, but to tell of what they discovered when they arrived there. The tomb, they found, was empty!

Now there could have been any number of reasons for the

missing corpse. One of them was the assumption made by Mary Magdalene, according to the Fourth Gospel, when she met Jesus outside the tomb and, thinking him to be a gardener, said, "Sir, if you removed him, tell me where you put him and I will take care of him." It would be a natural assumption, of course, that someone, for some reason, had removed the body. Matthew reports that the priests, faced with the same puzzling circumstance of the disappearance of the body of the man whom they had thought they had permanently silenced, spread the rumor that, in spite of the heavy guard at the tomb, Jesus' disciples had come and stolen it. Other possibilities might have been that the authorities themselves had removed the body, fearing that otherwise the tomb might have become a martyr's shrine; or that the women had been mistaken in identifying the tomb where Jesus had been buried. The explanation offered by the four Gospels, rather, was that God had raised Jesus from the dead.

It was not the empty tomb, however, that convinced the followers of Jesus of his resurrection. It was their own visionary experiences, or the reports of such experiences by others whom they trusted, that compelled them to believe that Jesus still lived. This can be seen in one of the earliest accounts of this history-changing event made by the Apostle Paul in the fifteenth chapter of his letter that is known as I Corinthians. In setting forth the evidence for the Resurrection as the basis of the Gospel that he preached he made no mention of the empty tomb, even though that might have given even more force to his argument. Instead he said,

I proclaimed, primarily, what I had been told, that Christ died for our sins, as the sacred writings had foretold, that he was buried and on the third day, was raised as those same writings predicted, and that he was seen by Peter and the rest of the Twelve. After that he was also seen by more than five hundred brothers at one time, the majority of whom remain alive though some have fallen asleep. Then, he was seen by James, then by all of the apostles, and lastly, as to one whose birth was overdue, he was even seen by me. (I Cor. 15:3-8)

By putting his own visionary experience of Christ, which is briefly described by himself in his Letter to the Galatians (1:15-16) and at more length, secondhand and several times in the Book of Acts, on the same level as that of the other Apostles, Paul implies that it was not a visitation by the corporeal body of Jesus, but a spiritual experience.

He gives more substance to this implication in the aforementioned resurrection chapter of I Corinthians (15), where he says of either Jesus' Resurrection, or the anticipated one of the believer following his or her demise:

"Someone may ask, 'How can the dead be raised? What kind of a body will they have?' Foolish questions! In planting seeds, you do not sow the full-grown plant, but only a bare seed, maybe of wheat or something else. But God gives it the body that He has provided, to each kind of seed its own kind of body. You know that all flesh is not the same: Human beings have one kind of flesh, animals another, birds another and fish another. There are heavenly bodies, as well as earthly ones, but the glory of the heavenly is of one kind, and that of the earthly is another. The sun has one kind of glory, the moon another, and the stars still another, and one star differs from another in glory. This is how it is with the resurrection. A perishable body is sown; an imperishable body is raised. It is sown in degradation; it is raised in grandeur. It is sown in its weakness; it is raised in matchless power. A natural body is buried in the earth, a spiritual body is raised to life eternal."

The Apostle's argument, of course, would have to be expressed somewhat differently in modern scientific terminology, but we can understand him. He is simply saying that after the resurrection the body is not the same. It is not a natural body. That was true of the body of Jesus, and it will be true of the body of the believer in the day of resurrection. It leaves us, then, with the same mystery: What happened to the (natural) body of Jesus?

Some might argue, and have argued, that Jesus' physical body, being made up, as is all other matter, of atoms, was subject to atomic disintegration. In most cases, this happens very slowly, but, in this one case, might have happened rapidly as it does in the atom bomb. This has even been offered as the explanation of the image of a man, assumed to be of Jesus, that appears on the supposed burial wrappings of Jesus, the Shroud of Turin. However, that particular evidence has been discounted by the more recent discovery that the Shroud, measured by the radioactive disintegration of carbon 14 found in it, is probably from about the fourteenth century AD. rather than the first. In any case, such a rapid disintegration of the body of Jesus into energy waves would have done much more than roll back the stone from the door of the tomb. It would have destroyed the whole tomb and most of the city of Jerusalem at the same time. So using the natural process of atomic disintegration as an explanation for the disappearance of the body of Jesus is not one that can be taken seriously.

A much more logical, and likely, explanation, aside from appealing to the supernatural, is that the body of Jesus was stolen from the tomb by someone, either his friends or enemies, and some other disposition made of it. With the tomb under heavy guard, and his disciples immobilized by fear of being taken into custody themselves, it is not likely to have been they who were responsible. If they had been, the subsequent firm faith of the same disciples and their friends in the reality of the resurrection would have been almost impossible to maintain. But, if the authorities, who, since they controlled the guards, were in position to have done it, had removed the body, then it was a big mistake that they made and one is left to wonder why they did not correct it by telling the truth when the stories of Jesus' resurrection began to arouse and motivate his followers to a renewed enthusiasm. So the question of what happened to the body of Jesus is, and is likely to remain, an insoluble mystery.

Perhaps the best conclusion we can draw is that proposed by Thomas Sheehan in his book, The First Coming: How the Kingdom of God Became Christianity. He wrote that no one really knows what happened to the body of Jesus. It really does not matter. Like the women who came to the tomb on the first Easter, we should go back to our normal every day lives and find there the meaning that Jesus taught us to find in them.[1]

In other words, the most positive and meaningful interpretation of the whole life-transforming experience was their "sensing" of his abiding presence as a Living Lord. Maybe that is why the first, and most notable, of the authors who recorded this experience, Paul of Tarsus, said nothing at all about the empty tomb. Nevertheless, the conviction of Jesus' followers, both men and women, that he had risen from the dead, is a remarkable testimony to the power of his personality. At first they could not believe that his enemies had killed him, and then they went on to a dynamic faith that in spite of that fact, he was still alive. Somehow, through the power of God, death had been overcome and he was still with them. This was the inner spiritual conviction that the reports of the outward phenomena of his post-Resurrection appearances, and the negative evidence of the empty tomb, were set forth to confirm.

Such powerful inner feelings are what often give rise to the mythopoeic tendencies of the human imagination. It may well be, then, that the best explanation of what happened following Jesus' death on the cross is to regard the whole confused and confusing account as the development of a myth. In a sense, therefore, we may consider that the Gospel accounts of Jesus' life and teachings begin and end in myths.

What Happened To The Body of Jesus?

Now many people of today's world misunderstand the meaning of myth. They think that it is just an untrue story; something that someone made up; simply fiction. To some extent that is true. It is a story that has been made up, but it is more than that. In both the Bible, and in classical Greek and Roman mythology, the myth is an attempt to express spiritual realities in material terms, cosmic truth in worldly language.

The use of myth for such a purpose was quite normal for writers living in a pre-scientific age, such as the time when the Bible, or the ancient traditions of almost any group of people around the world, were developed. They had some deep insights into the relationship of human beings with those who were their forebears, and with the world in which they found themselves, and they had no language in which to express such insights other than putting them into terms of the actions of gods, goddesses, and various superhuman powers and forces that they could perceive but not otherwise explain.

Other popular religions that were current in the Near East and throughout the Roman world in the first century made much of their myths of a dying and rising god, giving early Christianity, which was in competition with them, a strong incentive to develop similar myths of their own. One of the most popular at that time was a development of the very old Isis/Osiris myth that had come from ancient Egypt. Isis was a mother goddess who was moved by great grief over the violent death of her brother/husband, Osiris, to search out the dismembered parts of his body and restore him to life, making him king of the underworld where he judged the dead. A similar religion, based on a myth of a dying/rising deity, was the Eleusinian, in which the mother goddess, Demeter, effected the resurrection of her daughter, Persephone, in a myth that symbolized the new life of spring after the death of winter, thus anticipating the Christian celebration of Easter.

Other faiths or cults with similar themes were the Phrygian

mythology of Cybele/Attis, the Syrian one honoring Aphrodite/Adonis, and Persian Mithraism. All of these religions, which pervaded the world into which Christianity was born, were called mystery religions, so it is not surprising that Christianity started out by developing its own mystery.

The beginnings of the scientific revolution in the late sixteenth century, and its tremendous growth since then, has transformed our world and our life in it profoundly, and has made the mythological language much less meaningful, as we saw earlier in the chapter on "Where Is God?" Yet, it still does have meaning in terms of the relationships that it sought to express. We just have to translate it into language more appropriate to the world in which we live.

A post-World War I German theologian, Rudolf Bultmann, did this for the New Testament in particular in his books outlining a process of "demythologizing" these biblical writings.[2] His conclusions have not been generally accepted, perhaps partly because he tied them up with Existentialist philosophy, but they did provide a recognition of a very real fact, that much of the Bible is written in mythological language. This does not undermine the importance of Scripture, especially for anyone who has been exposed to the writings of the late Joseph Campbell. In his book, The Power of Myth, which has also been aired over public television through interviews with Bill Moyers, he says, for example, "The myths are metaphorical of spiritual potentiality in the human being, and the same powers that animate our life animate the life of the world." Also, "...the biblical tradition is socially oriented mythology."[3]

Legends are related to the mythmaking tendencies of the human imagination, but they deal with those who are authentic historical figures, and exaggerate their heroic qualities. An example of this is the well-known story of the youthful George Washington and the cherry tree. It is generally agreed that this is a story that was made up by an early American clergyman, Parson Weems, a preacher who used it as an illustration for a sermon point on the value of honesty. In the Bible, scholars agree, Elijah and Elisha were historical persons, members of the early prophetic order, prior to the writing prophets. But many of the stories told of them, with their supernatural overtones, are legendary. The same is true, we may well surmise, of many of the stories told of Jesus.

However, so great was the effect on the lives of those people who accepted his teachings by the narrative of a splendid life so quickly snuffed out, that they went beyond mere legendary exaggerations and sought to express their relationship to him, and to the God they believed had sent him, in myths of his miraculous birth and even more miraculous departure from his physical life. Quite possibly the Romans had him buried in a common unmarked grave, as they usually did with those who were executed by crucifixion, and the whole story of his burial in a borrowed tomb, by a secret, wealthy follower, assisted by a Pharisaic member of the Supreme Council, the Sanhedrin, was a part of the myth that was developed to explain his life.

----

[1] Thomas Sheehan, *The First Coming*, (New York: Dorset Press, 1986)

[2] Rudolf Karl Buthman, (1958) *Jesus Christ and Mythology*, (New York: esp. Chs. 1 and 3.

[3] Joseph Campbell (w. Bill Moyer), (1988) *The Power of Myth*, New York, p.p. 22,23.

CHAPTER SIX

JESUS AND THE KINGDOM OF GOD

(The Teachings of Jesus)

"He taught them, saying; '...This is the way you should pray:
'Our Father in heaven, may Your name be held in
reverence, may Your kingdom come, Your will be
done, on earth even as it is in heaven.'"

-Matthew 5:2, 6:9-10

As indicated in a previous chapter, the primary emphasis of
Jesus, when he began to preach in Galilee, was an announcement
of an imminent Kingdom of God. This is something that was
readily understood in the world of the first century, but something that cries out for explanation in the world of the
twenty-first century. We still know of kingdoms in our world, but
for the most part they are limited or constitutional monarchies.
With rare exceptions, kings and queens are usually figureheads in
our modern world. They serve a symbolic function representing
national identity and unity, and have some diplomatic value in
dealings with other nations, but the primary functioning of government rests with prime ministers or presidents and their cabi-
nets and with parliaments where all citizens of the country are
represented. But in Jesus' lifetime kings and emperors were often
absolute monarchs with little or no limitation on their powers of

government. That is the basis of Jesus' thinking when he announced an impending "Kingdom of God." He meant that God was about to assume absolute control in human, as in natural, affairs and His reign would be complete. God's kingdom, in other words, was not viewed in terms of territory to be embraced; though Jesus no doubt envisioned that territory as including the whole world and all of its people. His primary emphasis, however, was on the characteristics of God's reign, and that was the theme of his teaching.

However, the content of his teaching, even as the story of his life and deeds, has undergone considerable modification by the later organization of his followers, the church, which preserved the records of both. For several decades, at least, these teachings were passed along orally. The exact date when they were first written down is not certain. Mark's Gospel may have been written and circulated among Christian churches sometime between 65 and 75 AD, though there are scholars who propose a date as early as 60 AD, which would be only some three decades after the time that the events took place or Jesus' words were uttered. The other Gospels were likely written during the next three decades. Scholarly opinion generally assigns a date of between 75-85 AD to Matthew and 85-95 AD to Luke. Since the Gospel According to John makes statements that indicate a familiarity with the published letters of Paul and with the three Synoptic Gospels as well, its date is usually put as latest, between 95-110 AD, though there have been attempts to assign it a much earlier date.

Another source, beside Mark's Gospel, that was used by Matthew and Luke, is one that is titled "Q" from "quelle," the German word for "source." Whether it was written or simply an oral tradition of Jesus' teachings is not certainly known, since any trace of it outside of the two Gospels themselves has never been found. This was a collection of quotations from Jesus in the form of aphorisms, maxims, and parables, perhaps with some narrative settings or connective material. If written, it was earlier than either Matthew or Luke, since they both used it. One possibility is that it might have been published about the same time as Mark's Gospel, since he didn't use it, but another possibility is that it was never circulated in written form, but was an oral tradition of things that Jesus had said.

In any case this would have allowed sufficient time for certain traditions to develop around the ways in which the accounts of both Jesus' deeds and doctrines were passed on. These traditional ways have been analyzed under a careful, deductive discipline called "Form Criticism." It asserts that the accounts of Jesus' deeds and words were preserved, used, and interpreted to meet the needs of the body of believers during the years between when they were done or uttered, and the time when they were finally written down in the Gospel records. These were the needs of evangelism or sharing their beliefs about Jesus, of debate with their opponents, and of adjusting to the changing circumstances in the life of the Church, such as its moving out from the Jewish environment of Palestine into the more pagan environment of the Greco-Roman world.

Some of the forms in which the stories of Jesus' doings and teachings were passed on by the church until the time when they were finally written down in the Gospel records were: the older narratives, such as the Passion Story, probably derived from the teachings of the earliest Apostles; the collections of sayings without much indication as to the occasion on which they were made; the pronouncement stories, which were stories of a miracle or other incident ending with a remembered statement of Jesus; and the parables.

The parable is a form which many scholars believe most nearly preserves the original words of Jesus. A parable is a story which may or may not refer to an actual incident but which is very true to life; that is, it speaks to the recipients of the teaching in very lifelike and understandable terms and usually imparts a vivid picture. But the story is not an end in itself; it provides a window through which a deeper truth of a spiritual nature may be seen. Parables were not unusual in the world in which Jesus lived. Examples of them are to be seen in the Old Testament (e.g., the parable that the prophet Nathan told to King David II Samuel 12:14).

Other rabbis both before and after Jesus' time also made use of them. But the unique quality of Jesus' parables, as they are pre-served in the New Testament, are the vividness of the impression they make and the clever way in which they illustrate some deeper and more abstract truth.

Many of Jesus' parables deal with the central theme of his teachings, namely the Kingdom of God (Heaven.) But some of them also deal with qualities of life that might be expected of those who were eligible to live in that kingdom, such as a forgiv-ing attitude, sympathy, humility, compassion, and goodness or righteousness. In other words they were plainly intended to reveal some truths about the relationship between human beings and God, and, by extension, the ideal in their relationships to one another. From these we may well come to the conclusion that to the mind of Jesus the Kingdom of God was a realm in which right relationships prevailed. Those right relationships, summed up in Jesus' designation of two Old Testament commandments as being of prime importance: love of God, and love of one's fellow human beings, correspond to what we have previously called, Creative Relationship.

Parables, which illustrate these kind of relationships are: The Last Judgment (Matthew 25:31-46); The Lost Sheep (Matthew 18:12-14 and Luke 15:4-7); The Unmerciful Servant (Matthew 18:23-35); The Good Employer (Matthew 20:1-16); The Two Sons (Matthew 21:28-32); The Great Supper (Matthew 22:1-10 and Luke 14:16-24) The Prodigal Son (Luke 15:11-32); The Good

Samaritan (Luke 10:25-37); The Rich Man and Lazarus (Luke 16:19-31); The Unjust Steward (Luke 16:1-8); The Servant's Reward (Luke 17:7-10); The Unjust Judge (Luke 18:1-8) and The Pharisee and the Publican (Luke 18:9-14).

Creative relationships, illustrated in these parables, include: unselfish serving and God's love, forgiveness and mercy (illustrated negatively in the parable of The Unmerciful Servant,) as virtues which should be emulated by those who wish citizenship in God's Kingdom. Loving concern, obedience, shunning special privileges for any group of people, or any racial or religious prejudice; diligence, and humility are also urged.

Most of the parables, however, deal with different aspects of the Kingdom of God such as the time of its coming and the preconditions and preparations needed for that great event. When Jesus announced God's reign as being imminent, the natural question in the minds of those who listened was, "When?" All three Synoptic Gospels record that when Jesus foretold the destruction of the Temple in Jerusalem, the disciples came to him privately and asked, "When will this happen and what will be the signs of this prediction coming to pass?"[1] The answer given is in the form of a short apocalypse, a kind of writing that was very popular in the intertestamental period of Bible history. This may be, and very likely is, a later adaptation by the Church of a previous Jewish or, perhaps, a Christian prophet's writing, for its detailed setting forth of various historical, natural, and supernatural signs, including the parable of The Fig Tree, seem contradictory to the conclusion given: "Concerning that day or hour no one knows, not even the angels in heaven, or the Son, but only the Father. So beware! Keep alert! For you don't know when that time is coming!" This last bit of scripture gives the lie to the many modern predictors of the end of the world or the present age who try to base their predictions on a literal reading of scripture. Why is it that they don't take that verse literally?

Part of the preparation for the Kingdom's coming, of course, is being alert to its potentiality, as illustrated in the parable of the Ten Bridesmaids (Matthew 25:1-13); but it may also involve the meeting of certain preconditions for its coming, as is depicted in the parables of The Faithful and Unfaithful Slaves (Matthew 24:45-51, Luke 12:42-46) and The Talents (Matthew 25:14-30 and Luke 19:12-27). In other words the teachings of Jesus provide both an "interim ethic" and a "kingdom ethic." It is no temporary or future code for human behavior. It is one for right now, in the time and place where we are. Living in this way will bring in the Kingdom for it is already "within" or "among" you.[2]

Both Jesus and his disciples, as well as the people of Palestine who heard him, realized that his was a radical teaching. It involved a decisive break with the way they had been living, even for those who had strictly adhered to the Mosaic commandments and believed themselves to be righteous. That is why he laid down, as the first precondition for the coming of that Kingdom, "repent and believe the good news." (Matthew 4:17, Mark 1:15). To repent meant to "turn around," to go in a new direction, and in his subsequent teaching, the good news or Gospel, he set forth that new direction in a wealth of specific detail. Believe this, and live by it, he was saying, and the longed for Kingdom will come; the New Age will dawn. Repentance and trust were the basic requirements.

The nature of that new way of living is given in the teachings of Jesus that were summed up in collections of his sayings, such as the Sermon on the Mount (Matthew chapters 5, 6, and 7), and Luke's version of the same or similar event, The Sermon on the Plain (Luke 6:20-49). The fact that some parallels to the sayings in Matthew's collection are found scattered throughout Luke's Gospel is an indication that these were things that were not said simply on one occasion, but throughout Jesus' period of ministry. Matthew, it would seem, brought them together into one part of his Gospel in what may have been a conscious attempt to portray Jesus as a new Moses, laying down the laws of a new covenant. Luke's version also seems more primitive, and thus more original, in its presentation of these aphorisms and maxims. For example, Matthew's eight beatitudes (Matthew 5:3-12) are paralleled in Luke by four beatitudes and four woes (Luke 6:20-26). In addition Luke's beatitudes are more straightforward and unembellished, while Matthew's may be best described as spiritualized.³ Matthew's version seems more likely to have been derived from something like Luke's quotation than the other way around, even though most Christians of today, as Matthew's original readers did, generally find his rendering more pleasing. One thing should be perfectly obvious to the careful reader of these collections of the sayings of Jesus that are found in both Matthew and Luke. This is that they deal with the relationships between persons, either with other people, or with the Supreme Person, God. Mention has been made in a previous chapter of the radical revision that Jesus urged in human relationships, especially in the area of dealing with one's enemies. Similar departures from the commonly accepted norms of human behavior, in his time and ours, make up much of the rest of the Sermon on the Mount (Matthew) or Sermon on the Plain (Luke). For example, he adds to the Mosaic commandment against murder an instruction to avoid anger and insults. To the one against adultery he adds a recommendation to curb the lustful look and reinforces it by saying, "If your right eye causes you to sin, pluck it out, and if your right hand causes you to sin, cut it off." He also repeals an Old Testament provision for divorce under certain circumstances and forbids oath taking as being unnecessary for one who is habitually honest.

In our relationship to God Jesus has some words about the privacy and secrecy of real prayer that are given little heed by his self-professed truest followers of today who want vocal praying of Christian prayers in schools and other public gatherings. He has similar things to say about fasting, which in our affluent and self-indulgent society is not a practice frequently cherished even by those same true followers.[4]

In between these two recommendations Matthew also inserts the very familiar and oft-repeated Lord's Prayer as an example of what prayer ought to be, brief and to the point. Luke, in a different setting, gives an even shorter version of this prayer, and even Mark's Gospel makes reference to some of its petitions. Matthew's version is particularly notable because it draws a parallel that helps to define what God's Kingdom is: "Your kingdom come, Your will be done, on earth even as it is in heaven." In answer to the frequent question, "When will God's Kingdom come?" this quotation might well lead us to conclude: "It has come and will come, again and again, whenever God's will is done." On the other hand it has not yet come in its completeness, and may never come in that sense, in the life of humanity on Earth.

In connection with the concept of God's imminent kingdom, the question naturally arises, in the Gospels themselves as well as in subsequent Church doctrine, what was Jesus' connection with the kingdom that he announced? The three Synoptic Gospels all report that Jesus, himself, posed the question of his identity to his closest followers. On their way to the northern Palestinian district of Caesarea Philippi, where the epiphany of the Transfiguration was to take place about a week later, he asked, "Who are people saying that I am?"

They answered with some of the opinions that they had overheard: "John the Baptist or Elijah, or one of the other prophets has returned."

Then Jesus questioned, "But who do you say that I am?"

Then Peter, alone, had an answer, "You are the Christ (i.e., the expected Messiah)." Only Matthew records Jesus' response to Peter's confession of faith, "Blessed are you, Simon, son of Jonah, for flesh and blood has not revealed this to you, but my Father in heaven."

Then, in Matthew, follows that commissioning of Peter as the leader of the still to be founded Church, "on this rock I will build my church, and the powers of death shall not prevail against it." That, together with the statement about the keys of the kingdom, sounds like a later addition by the Church, and probably is an effort to legitimize its authority.

In Matthew's version, also, is found a phrase, which is frequently on the lips of Jesus in the Synoptics as his self-identification: "Who do people say that the Son of Man is?" The term, although a common one in the Gospels, is an ambiguous one. Why this circumlocution? Son of Man, literally, means a human being of course. It is a direct opposite to Son of God, which, as we have already seen, Christianity later applied to him. But scholars point out that the phrase was not original with Jesus. It had a long history.

In the Book of Ezekiel, written probably six centuries before Jesus was born, the prophet in his visions and audiences with God was commonly addressed as "son of man" (ben adam), meaning, obviously, a human being, a mortal. In the prophetic Book of Daniel, published around four centuries later, heavenly beings are described as resembling or having the appearance of "sons of men." Subsequent intertestamental literature made use of the phrase to describe a figure called variously the Elect One, the Anointed One, or the Son of Man. He was to serve as God's agent in the Day of the Lord, or the final victory of good over evil, which is also characterized in some of these writings as "the manifestation of the Son of Man."

It could be, then, that either Jesus himself, or the Gospel writers, were using this as a cryptic identification of him with a mysterious messianic figure. In any case it appears that Jesus had a different concept in mind, if Luke's version of the beginning of his ministry by an announcement in the synagogue of his home-town, Nazareth, may be regarded as authentic. He simply quoted the noble words of the third author to be included in the biblical book of Isaiah, as his own concept of his mission.[5] However, since this announcement is not supported by parallel passages in the other Synoptic Gospels, it is far from certain that Jesus did use it. Nevertheless it cannot be denied that, even in those parallel passages, Jesus thought of himself primarily as a prophet sent to announce a new day for Israel.

Another concept, however, which could have been part of Jesus' self-identification is that of the "suffering servant." This is a concept, which arose and was eloquently expressed in the writings of the otherwise unknown prophet, called "Deutero-Isaiah," which are found in the lengthy book of Isaiah in chapters 40 to 55. In that context the "Suffering Servant" plainly represents a personification of the people of Israel, who had just returned (at least some of them) from the bitter experience of exile in Babylon. It was an attempt, and a notably successful one, on the part of the author of this portion of scripture, to interpret what God was trying to do in permitting the suffering of the exilic experience to occur to his "chosen people."

That the concept of servanthood (or slavery) was especially meaningful to Jesus is indicated in the fact that the servant (or slave) is a prominent figure in some of his parables.[6] He is even reported to have said, "The Son of Man came not to be served but to serve, and to give his life a ransom for many" (Mk. 10:45; Matt. 20:28). Just before this he had said to the two sons of Zebedee, who had come seeking prominent positions in his coming kingdom: "...whoever wishes to become great among you must be your servant, and whoever wishes to be first among you must be slave of all." This indicates that the Kingdom he had come to announce was a Kingdom of Service, and he was among them as the chief servant (or slave.)

Even so, Jesus, who was completely familiar with the writings in the Book of Isaiah, as well as with the stories of the martyred prophets, when the time came for his confrontation with the leaders of Judaism and their pagan overlords, could hardly avoid thinking of himself as the Suffering Servant, the one in whom the mission of Israel had come to focus. Therefore he is quoted saying, "Yet today, tomorrow and the next day I must be on my way, because it is impossible for a prophet to be killed outside of Jerusalem" (Luke 13:33), and he "set his face" to go to that city (Luke 9:51). Many of his actions from that time on, either consciously or unconsciously, carried out the imagery of the Servant Songs of II Isaiah.[7]

Looking at the gospel record, then, of what Jesus said in the light of what he did, it becomes quite clear that, in the originality of his thought, he set forth a new interpretation for many of the concepts that had developed over the centuries in his inherited religion of Judaism and proposed a radical reform in the way people should conceive of their religion and put it into practice. A central novelty of his approach to the realm of religious thought and action was his emphasis on the prime importance of human relationships. The God he worshiped and served, though so far as we know he never put it into just these words, was a God of Creative Relationships.

---

[1] Matthew 24:3, Mark 13:4, and Luke 21:7.

[2] C.f., Luke 17:21.

[3] For example, Luke's version says, "Blessed are you who are poor, for the Kingdom of God is yours," but Matthew's rendering is, "Blessed are the poor in spirit; for the Kingdom of God belongs to them.

[4] Matthew 6:5-8, 16-18..

[5] This writer is designated by scholars as Trito-Isaiah.

Jesus and the Kingdom of God

6 e.g.,(Mk. 13:34-36; Lk. 12:35-38); (Matt. 24:45-51; Lk. 12:41-45); (Matt. 18:22-35); Matt. 25:14-30; Lk. 19:11-27); (Lk. 16:1-8) and (Lk. 17:7-10).

7 Isaiah 42:1-4; 49:1-6; 50:4-9 and 52:13 - 53:12.

CHAPTER SEVEN

GOD IN US
(The Holy Spirit)

It was noted back in the second chapter of this book, where we dealt with the question "Where is God?" that many anthropologists believe that human religion had its origin in the concept of vaguely defined spirits, or mysterious powers that animated many phenomena in the world of nature, either living or nonliving. This is a basic religious belief that the scientific study of human origins and development calls animism. As the mind evolved with increasing brain capacity in various human species and individuals began to distinguish themselves from the world around them, they perceived powers in the natural environment, which seemed to resemble the powers that animated them. They began to revere or to fear such powers in accord with whether they perceived them to be helpful or threatening, i.e., good or evil.

We also noted in that chapter the progressive personifying of such spirits of good or evil in later gods and goddesses, who populated the unseen spiritual world around them, along with the more familiar and predictable material world where they found themselves. These gods and goddesses may have dwelt in some isolated natural realm like the summit of a high mountain (e.g., Mount Olympus), but they could disguise themselves and wander among human habitations as well, or send messenger spirits or angels to carry their instructions or accomplish their purposes in human affairs.

In the Hebrew-Christian tradition that is reflected in our Bible, though the idea of one supreme God who created and controlled all things gradually prevailed, the concept of a divine spirit by which He accomplished his will remained in the human religious imagery. For instance the story of creation in the first chapter of Genesis pictures the Spirit of God, or a mighty wind of divine origin, sweeping over the original chaotic watery abyss. This reminds us that in early human thought the power of the unseen wind gave a naturalistic basis for spiritual power. Thus in both the Hebrew "ruach" and the Greek "pneuma" the word for wind also became the word for spirit. Even in that descriptive passage in the Acts of the Apostles where the evangelist Luke records the coming of the Holy Spirit upon the disciples in accord with a promise Jesus had made, he uses the imagery of "the sound of a mighty wind," to picture it.[1] Another image for the Holy Spirit is also included in the same passage, "tongues as of fire" which descend upon the Apostles giving them an extraordinary eloquence in many languages. Both wind and fire were natural phenomena that filled human minds with awe as they still do when a hurricane or tornado strikes, a volcano erupts or a forest burns. The difference is that we now understand the natural causes behind these phenomena and can do something to control or to avoid their destructive power, while in ancient times they seemed to have an origin and power for destruction far beyond human understanding.

A notable advance in the concept of the spirit and its function is found both in the Gospel According to John, and in the Letters of Paul. In the former Jesus is portrayed as sharing a deep insight with a sinful woman of Samaria (in Jewish eyes somewhere near the lowest of the low in spiritual capacity). In answer to her question, as to the proper place of worship, whether it was the

Jerusalem Temple, or the Samaritan one on Mount Gerizim, he is quoted as saying, "Woman, believe me, a time is coming when God, the Father, will not be worshipped either on this mountain or in Jerusalem. The true way to salvation is handed down in Jewish tradition, for they have a fuller revelation of who and what God is, but the day in which all worshippers shall worship Him in spirit and truth has already come and, indeed, God seeks such worshippers wherever they may be found. God is Spirit and those who worship Him must do so in spirit and in truth."[2] In the latter case, the prolific writer Paul deals at length with the role of the Holy Spirit in worship and in life, and lists both the gifts and the fruits of the Spirit, as well as ways to attain a spirit- filled life both in this world and in the future resurrection. Going beyond what the Synoptic Gospel writers did, in portraying what Jesus had to say about God's realm or kingdom, Paul connected this to the life inspired by the Holy Spirit. In writing to the Roman Christians, in connection with various Jewish or early Christian dietary regulations, he advised that they should not be judgmental of the practices of others, nor should they allow what they ate or drank to become a barrier or give offense to others. Instead, he wrote: "Do not let what you consider good become evil in the sight of others, for God's kingdom is not a matter of eating or drinking, but rather of righteousness, peace and joy in the Holy Spirit. Serving Christ in this way is not only pleasing to God but approved by other people."[3]

Both Paul and the writer of the Fourth Gospel thought of the Holy Spirit as a divine empowerment not only coming upon persons at rare intervals, as in the Old Testament, but as an abiding manifestation of the revelation and power of God in the life of the Christian. That Spirit which had imbued and motivated Jesus during his earthly life had remained after that physical life had come to an end, and inspired and empowered his followers in obeying his teachings and continuing his ministry. In the interval between his first coming, and his anticipated return (regarded as being only a short time by his earliest followers) the Holy Spirit would be the agency through which both God and Christ would continue to be with them and affect their lives. It was in this sense, then, that the Apostle Paul could enumerate the gifts of the Spirit in I Corinthians 12, and pronounce "agape," love, to be the greatest spiritual gift in I Corinthians 13. Jesus, himself, in such authentic teachings as we may be able to derive from the Synoptic Gospels, does little to advance any doctrine of the Holy Spirit. He seems to have thought of the spirit that animated and inspired the prophets of the Old Testament as the motivating power in his own life. According to Luke's Gospel, he began his ministry in Nazareth by quoting from the anonymous prophet whose words are recorded in the third section of the Book of Isaiah: "The Lord's Spirit is upon me, anointing me to announce good news to the poor, freedom for captives, sight to the blind, and release for the downtrodden, thus proclaiming the year of the Lord's favor."[4]

One observation, most likely authentic, concerning the Holy Spirit is found in Matthew 12:31-32, where, in response to the Pharisaic criticism that he might be empowered by Beelzebul, the Prince of Demons, rather than by God, he said, "I tell you all sin and blasphemy may be forgiven except blasphemy against the Spirit. So denunciation of me as a human being will be forgiven, but denunciation of the Holy Spirit will not be forgiven." Here, as in Luke 4:18-19, Jesus expresses the thought that the motivating power in his life was the Holy Spirit, the dynamic of God's inner presence. But Luke also goes on in his second volume on early Christian history, the Book of Acts, to connect to this inner dynamic that was in Jesus the dynamic of the early church in carrying on his mission. In Luke's Gospel the motivating power of Jesus is expressed in and through remarkable deeds of compassion: healing many who were sick or handicapped; the acceptance of outcasts such as Levi or Zacchaeus into his circle of friendship; accepting women, who were regarded as subservient to men throughout most of society in that time into the fellowship of his followers; accepting invitations into the homes of even his opponents and critics, the Pharisees; expressing forgiveness from the cross for those who crucified him and promising salvation to a repentant criminal being crucified beside him.

True, many of these stories he shares with the other Gospel writers, Matthew and Mark, but not all of them, and in many respects Luke seems to heighten the magnanimity of Christ's spirit. In Acts, his history of the early years of the developing community of believers in Jesus as Messiah and Lord, moreover, he goes on to portray the disciples' power to overcome obstacles and do miraculous deeds of healing or remarkable feats of oratory through that same Holy Spirit.

Is there, we might well ask, any scientific basis for this phenomenon of the Holy Spirit that was so central to the Christian Community in the first century, and which is still with us, especially in the Pentecostal Churches, as we move into the twenty-first century? Whatever reality this so-called spiritual dynamic does have in societies and individuals today, we must conclude, is to be found in the mind of the believer or believers who exhibit it. As we have seen, the imagery of a divine wind or fire is not acceptable in our day when natural explanations of such phenomena are plain. And, as we noted in the second chapter, such concepts may indeed go back to the most primitive theological speculations that entered the mind of humanity when humans were just becoming conscious of the relationship between the self, the universe, and its inhabitants.

On the other hand, thoughts and ideas in the minds of individuals obviously often motivate them to overcome great obstacles or bear a great deal of mental or physical suffering in order to carry out goals to which they are deeply committed.

146

For some of them this empowerment is attributed to an indwelling power of God, or to the Holy Spirit, which gives them greater resources of strength, determination, and staying power than they would otherwise have. This, rather than a simple altruism or will to the greatest good, mentioned in Chapter 1 is "God in Us," Creative Relationship at work in our personal lives. So-called miraculous powers or the ability to become fluent in languages one has never learned, then, are less the work of God than they are ecstatic phenomena that sometimes animated even pagan oracles and seers. Paul of Tarsus, who had a fine logical mind, even though one that was committed to the religious insights of his Hebrew ancestors, was wise enough to downgrade such spiritual gifts and make them subservient to the all-important gift of love, Creative Relationship.[5]

In another of his letters to churches, Paul listed qualities of life, which he designated as fruits of the Spirit, in distinguishing them from the gifts of the Spirit. These fruits of the spirit-filled life he listed as love, joy, peace, patience, kindness, goodness, faithfulness, humility and self-control. These are surely the positive characteristics of persons, which we might confirm as being creative relationships. He makes this even more apparent by listing their opposites, the destructive relationships, or sins, such as immorality, obscenity, indecency, idolatry, trickery, enmity, hatred, divisiveness, anger, jealousy, and drunkenness with orgies.[6] Plainly, for Paul, the Spirit-filled life was one that was under control, and that control was a mind dominated by Creative Relationship, or God in Us.

---

[1] Acts 2:1-4.

[2] John 4:21-24.

[3] C.f. Romans 14:13-18.

[4] C.f., Luke 4:18-19 (Isaiah 61:1-2). Scholars generally divide

the Book of Isaiah among three prophets: Isaiah of Jerusalem (742-700 B.C.E.),Chs. 1-39; Deutero-Isaiah (c. 540 BC), Chs. 40-55; and Trito-Isaiah (after 538 BC) Chs. 56-66.

[5] C.f., I Corinthians 12, 13, and 14.

[6] Galatians 5:19-23.

CHAPTER EIGHT

PROPHETS AND PROFITS

"Where true religion has prevented one crime, false religions have afforded a pretext for a thousand."

-Colton

It is generally agreed today, as it was even prior to the coming of Jesus, that the highest manifestation of religion is to be found in the "writing prophets"[1] of the Hebrew tradition preserved in the Old Testament, and in particular those who were proclaiming their message in the eighth century before Christ. These, as we have seen in the chapter immediately preceding this one, were believed to be possessed by the divine spirit in an especially great measure. Their evaluation of the purposes and practices of religion in that early time still serve to give us a standard by which to measure the value and effectiveness of religious practices today.

We can get the flavor of their sermons, in reading the short books of Amos, Hosea, and Micah from the Hebrew Book of the Twelve as translated in our modern English Bibles. The first of these in the order of the biblical canon is Hosea, but he was not the first chronologically. That honor belongs to Amos, a "shepherd" and "dresser of fig trees," who traveled from his native Judah, the southern kingdom of divided Israel, to the northern kingdom sometime around 750 B.C.E. A short distance beyond the border between the two kingdoms he came to Bethel, the site of an important religious shrine of the northern kingdom, Israel, where he preached outside the temple erected by King Jeroboam I about a century and a half earlier, and there he predicted the fall of the kingdom.

O Israelites, the people that He brought out of the land of Egypt, hear the charge that Yahweh brings against you: 'You only of all the families on earth, have I known and loved; Therefore, I will punish you for all your sins.'[2]

Another diatribe follows:
Listen, and bear witness against Jacob's house,
for this is the word of Yahweh, God of hosts:
'On the day when I punish Israel for its waywardness,
I will destroy the altars of Baal; the horns of the altar shall be cut off and fall to the ground.
I will wreak havoc on both the winter house and
the summer house, and ivory houses shall disappear entirely.
Many great houses will be wiped out. The word of Yahweh!'[3]

Subsequent chapters in the Book of Amos reemphasize the prophet's dire warnings wherein he contrasts the prosperity and luxury of the kingdom of Israel in the days of Jeroboam II with the plight of their ancestors, slaves who had fled from Egypt and wandered through the desert solely dependent on the mercy of God for food and safety. His oratory is magnificent as he castigates the people and their rulers:
Seek Yahweh and survive, or else He will break out like fire in Joseph's house and spread throughout Bethel, with no one to quench it.
O you who turn justice to bitterness,
and trample righteousness under foot!

He who made the Pleiades and Orion,
Who turns the darkness of midnight into
morning light, and again turns day into night,
Who summons the waters of the sea,
and spreads them out over the land,
Yahweh is his name,
Who causes disaster to break forth against the strong, and
destruction to rain down on the fortress."

. . .

Seek good and not evil,
that you may survive
So the Lord, the God of hosts, will be with you,
as you have said.
Hate evil and love good,
and establish justice at the gate:
Then it may be that the Lord, the God of hosts,
will be gracious to the remnant of Joseph.[4]

It is not surprising, then, that Amaziah, the priest of Bethel, took offense at this character who stood outside the door of the sanctuary and denounced it and the whole kingdom so comprehensively. According to the 7th chapter of Amos, the priest sent a message to King Jeroboam II saying, "Amos has conspired against you in the very center of the house of Israel; the land is not able to bear all his words."

Prophets, however, were highly respected as holy men in Israel and Judah, and even rulers hesitated to take action against them. They were regarded as spokesmen for the deity himself.[5] Therefore even kings did not dare to take rash action against the prophets, even though many exceptions tested this rule, and prophecy could only be regarded as a hazardous occupation. In a lengthy sermon, apparently circulated among Jewish (Hebrew) Christians in the late first or early second centuries after the

Church was founded, the unknown writer proclaims the exploits of the heroes of the faith as recorded in the Old Testament. Of the prophets he writes:

"Some were subjected to mockery and whippings; others to chains and imprisonment. They were stoned to death, tortured, sawn in two, slain with the sword. They went around in sheep and goat skins, destitute, oppressed and mistreated—men of whom the world was not worthy—wandering in deserts and mountains and living in caves and holes in the ground."[6]

Though a contemporary of Amos, the prophet Hosea, whose career is reviewed in the first of the shorter prophetic Books of the Twelve, seems to have been a native of the northern kingdom, and not from the Kingdom of Judah, as was Amos. He began his prophesying during the reign of the same Jeroboam II, to whom the priest of the sanctuary at Bethel, Amaziah, had complained of that fiery prophet's apparently seditious sermons. Hosea, however, though he pulled no punches in his denunciations of the evils of Israelite society, was not quite the harbinger of doom that Amos had been. The difference was perhaps due to the personal marital experiences of Hosea, in which he found a paradigm of God's relationship to Israel.

The details of his troubled marriage are difficult to unravel in the prophet's book, since the focus of his message was on the religious and political situation in Israel, rather than on his own domestic difficulties. But, apparently, after his own disrupted relationship with the mother of his children, Hosea found a deeper understanding of God's relationship to Israel: divine love for his wayward consort, Israel, whom he had brought out of slavery in Egypt and made into his own Chosen People. In spite of their departure from the covenant made with Israel under Moses, God was ready to forgive them if they would repent and return to him. Hosea had found that he still loved his wife, Gomer, enough, even after her infidelity, to go and buy her back from a life of prostitution and restore her to the family relationship. Would God do less for Israel?

Hosea's guarded optimism, relying on God's love for Israel, in spite of the infidelity of its people, was not the way things happened for them. During the reign of Hoshea, some fifteen years after the death of Jeroboam II, the death of the Assyrian Emperor, Tiglath-Pileser III, took place (727 B.C.E.) and the Israelite monarch, Hoshea, took that event as an opportunity to revolt and stop paying the annual tribute that Israel had been rendering to the Assyrian Empire. He hoped that a resurgent Egypt would back him up in this daring political venture.

Hoshea, however, both underestimated the Assyrian dynasty's ability to overcome the crisis, and overestimated the power of a weak Egyptian pharaoh to do anything to help Israel. A new emperor, Shalmaneser V, quickly attacked Samaria. A gleam of hope came to the Israelites when this monarch was killed in battle, but he was quickly succeeded by Sargon II, who finished the campaign and, after a three-year siege, took Samaria. Sargon's own record of the victory says that he deported 27,290 Israelites into the region of Persia which was also under Assyrian domination, and repopulated Israel with colonists from Babylonia, Elam, and Syria. So far as we know Hosea did not live to see his hopeful prophecy fail and the tragedy foreseen by his predecessor, Amos, come true, but his words were preserved and cherished in the southern kingdom of Judah which alone survived.

The third of the triumvirate of the eighth century BC so-called minor prophets was Micah, a native of the southern kingdom of Judah, about whose life and the circumstances of his prophecies little is known. Apparently he came on the religio-political scene some twenty to thirty years after the time of Amos and Hosea, and preached primarily in the southern kingdom of Judah rather than in Israel as they had done. A note in Jeremiah 26:18, which quotes from Micah 3:12, says that he prophesied during the reign of King Hezekiah of Judah, who ruled from 715 to 687 BC. The introduction to his book in the Bible says that he also was active during the reigns of Hezekiah's two predecessors, Jotham and Ahaz, which would make him a contemporary of Amos and Hosea. However, his message, originating in and directed primarily to the southern kingdom, was greatly overshadowed by that of his towering contemporary, Isaiah of Jerusalem.

Isaiah, who is designated as one of the major prophets, was a sophisticated urban dweller, a familiar figure in the courts of Jerusalem's kings, and a worshiper in its Temple of Solomon. In that he is quite a contrast to Micah who came from a small village, Moreshethgath, about twenty-five miles southwest of Jerusalem, and who spent no small portion of his time and energy in denouncing life in the big cities of Samaria in the north and Jerusalem in the south.[7]

As a member of the priestly aristocracy[8] who centered his prophetic activities in the capital of the southern kingdom, Judah, rather than in the northern kingdom of Israel, Isaiah's message differed considerably from that of his contemporaries, Amos, Hosea and Micah. Like another major prophet, Jeremiah, who appeared on the scene in Palestine about a century later, Isaiah didn't spend much time denouncing the rulers of the land. Both of these prophets may have felt that the troubled international situation gave the monarchs enough problems without their adding to the burdens. Most of Jeremiah's activity as a prophet was during the reign of Josiah, the good king who established the Deuteronomic Reform in Judaism, while the latter part of Isaiah's career was during the reign of Hezekiah, an energetic and pious king, who carried through an earlier religious reform as well as building up the defenses of Jerusalem. Nevertheless, in neither case did these prophets hesitate to criticize and to warn of the consequences of certain of the king's foreign policies.

In all instances, however, a major element in the message of the eighth century prophets was a focus on the religion of the people, including the king and his courtiers. They denounced the apostasy of the inhabitants of land, including their religious and political leaders, and their departure from the ethical standards of the Mosaic law and a concern for each other learned from their experiences as wanderers in the desert of Sinai. In the prophet's eyes the prosperity of the land of Israel (the northern kingdom) had corrupted their religion. Priest and ruler, alike, had opted for a religion of showy ritual and ceremonial requirements and had downgraded the ethical and moral standards that had characterized the religion of Moses and their own forebears who had followed Joshua into the land with the words, "As for me and my family, we will serve the Lord" (Joshua 24:15).

When it came to religion and what kind of worship God wanted from his people, the words of the eighth century prophets made it crystal clear:

I hate, I scorn your feasts, and I take no
pleasure in your formal ceremonies.
Even though you bring me burnt offerings and
cereal offerings,
I will not accept them;
and the thank offerings of your fatted cattle,
I will not notice them.
Go away from me with the noise of your songs; I will
not listen to the melody of your instruments.
But, let justice roll down like waters, and righteousness like
an ever-flowing stream"
(Amos 5:21-24)
Even though Ephraim built many altars
for penitence,
they have become to him altars for sinning.
Were I to write for him my laws by the thousands,
they would be regarded by him as meaningless.

Creative Relationship

They love to make sacrifices; they gladly eat
the roasted flesh,
but Yahweh has no delight in them.
Rather He will remember their iniquity,
and punish their sins:
they shall go back to Egypt.
For Israel has forgotten his Maker and built palaces;
while Judah has multiplied fortified cities.
But I will send a fire upon his cities,
and it shall devour his fortresses.
(Hosea 8:11-14)

'With what shall I come before the Creator,
and bow down before God most high?
Shall I come before him with burnt offerings,
with calves a year old?
Will God be happy with thousands of rams,
and ten thousand rivers of oil?
Shall I give my firstborn for my transgression,
the fruit of my body for the sin of my soul?'
He has shown you, O man, what is good;
What does your Creator require of you
but to do justice, and to love mercy,
and to walk humbly with your God?"
(Micah 6:6-8)

"What to me is the multitude of your sacrifices?"
says Yahweh;
"I have had too many burnt offerings of rams
    and too much fat from overfed cattle;
I do not delight in the blood of bulls,
    or of lambs, or of male goats.
When you come to appear before me,

Who requires of you this trampling of my courts?
Bring no more vain offerings;
    incense is an abomination to me.
New moon and sabbath and the calling of assemblies—
I cannot endure iniquity and solemn assembly.
Your new moons and your appointed feasts my soul hates;
  they have become a burden to me,
I am weary of bearing them.
  When you spread forth your hands, I will hide my
  eyes from you;
Even though you make many prayers, I will not listen;
    your hands are full of blood.
  Wash yourselves; make yourselves clean;
  remove the evil of your doings from before my eyes;
  stop doing evil; learn to do good;
  seek justice, correct oppression;
  defend the fatherless, plead for the widow."
(Isaiah 1:11-17)

After reading their words uttered in the eighth century before our era, it is not too difficult to imagine what these prophets of God might have to say about our modern institutional Christianity with its cathedrals and elaborate church buildings; or about its masses and liturgies, doctrinal squabbles, and debates over polity. If, as we have asserted, the nature and activity of God in our world and universe is that of Creative Relationship, then why must the church be the cause of divisions rather than harmony? Why should it spend so much time and energy in trying to determine who belongs in its organizations, and relatively so little effort in trying to win people to God's way of establishing and enhancing our values through creative relationships?

As has been said earlier, too much of modern Christianity is devoted to a religion about Jesus and too little to the religion of

Jesus, for he was in the line of the prophets, and lived by their insights. Recall the story of his driving out the moneychangers and the sellers of the sacrificial animals from the courtyard of the Jerusalem Temple, and quoting, as his justification for such an action, words from Isaiah (56:7) and Jeremiah (7:11): "Is it not written: 'My house shall be called a house of prayer for all nations,' but you have made it a 'den of robbers.'" He, too, saw the sacrificial system as it developed in later Judaism as a religious racket for raising money for the temple and its staff and not a means of communication with God.

In traveling in Europe, I have seen for myself the magnificent art and architecture that was put into the great churches and cathedrals, by which the people were told that they could honor God and win His favor. I have seen the isolated monasteries with bare cells for the monks, but chapels awash with marble and gold leaf supposedly for the glory of God.

Jesus and the prophets would have said that God would be honored more in what they might have used their resources to do for some of the poor and sick and starving, than in such shows of piety. History reminds us that Pope Leo X raised money for the magnificent palace of the Vatican, decorated with Michelangelo's matchless art, by conducting a scam throughout Europe selling indulgences, which were actually advance absolution for the populace to commit the sins proscribed by the Church. Unfortunately this pope, whose fund-raising efforts gave rise to the Protestant Reformation by arousing the righteous indignation and prophetic passion of Martin Luther, was neither the first nor the last religious racketeer, using the devotion of the faithful to advance their own wealth, prestige, and power. Modern technologies, such as television, have enabled the unscrupulous to raise that demonic art to new heights.

What flights of vehement oratory might be heard from an Amos or Isaiah if they were alive in our world today? What greater depths of anguish must be thrust upon our crucified Savior as he sees how far today's religion about Him departs from the truth that He taught?

Televangelists of today are using modern technologies of communication and well-developed techniques of fund raising to further their own power and prestige in the secular world. Ignoring or even actively opposing our country's laws to prevent the church and the state from interfering in the affairs of each other, they strive to induce legislators to pass laws which will promote their particular brand of religion, and give the state, which they hope to control, power to use tax funds to support religious institutions.

The First Amendment to the United States Constitution provides, among other freedoms, that the government shall not establish (which means give official sanction to) institutional religion nor forbid the free exercise of religion by an individual citizen or groups of citizens, and it has worked marvelously well for both the good of the state and the good of the churches, synagogues, and religious societies for more than two centuries.

Religion today is still what it was in the days of the prophets and of Jesus: a commitment by the individual to the idea of Creative Relationship in both personal and group life as the Way of God for our world. Any religion that seeks to exploit or manipulate people for whatever purpose is a false religion!

---

[1] Excerpts from their sermons, delivered orally, were written down either by the prophets themselves or by scribes among their disciples who recorded their words.

[2] Amos 3:1, 2.

[3] Ibid., 3:13, 15.

[4] Op cit., 5:6-9; 14, 15.

[5] The Hebrew word, "nabi," meant spokesperson, after the

fashion of Aaron in Exodus 4:14-16, who was made the "nabi" for Moses in speaking to the Egyptian pharaoh.

[6] Hebrews 11:36-38.

[7] C.f., Micah 1:5, 6; 1:9; 3:1-4; 9-12.

[8] Little information is given in the Bible concerning the lineage and youth of Isaiah, son of Amoz, but this much may be surmised from his familiarity with the Temple and its ritual, and his ready acceptance in the courts of the Judean kings.

CHAPTER NINE

THE END OF TIME

"Heaven and earth will pass away, but my words will by no means do so.

Yet, concerning the day and hour, no one knows, not the messengers of God in heaven, nor I, but only the Father."

—Jesus, (Matthew 24:35-36.)

One of the characteristics of humans, probably as far back as the beginning of their knowledge that one day succeeds another, was to be anxious about what tomorrow might bring. Remembering the past has always led us to wondering about the future. Therefore no commandment of Jesus is harder to heed than when he said, in his Sermon on the Mount, "Don't be anxious about tomorrow, for tomorrow will have its own anxieties. Let the troubles of each day be sufficient for it"(Matt. 6:34).

The people who lived in Bible times were no exception to this human tendency to be concerned and to speculate about what each new day might bring into their lives. In the previous chapter, we have seen that the prophets led them to think about what the trials and triumphs of the present might bring to pass in the future. Gradually this led them to wonder about the ultimate goal of history.

Other peoples of the earth, for example the Hindu people of India, pictured history as being cyclic in nature, an endless cycle of birth, death and rebirth. They sought escape from this essentially meaningless cycle by various means, one of which was found in the teachings of Gautama Buddha, c.538 B.C.E., who showed how one might attain a higher spiritual state of nirvana.

The Hebrew people, on the other hand, looked at history as a progression. There was a future goal toward which humanity moved by steps outlined in a God-given law, or in the teachings of prophets or philosophers. True, there was, in this life, strife and bloodshed, suffering and misery, but they believed a way could be found, or would be revealed, that would lead ultimately to a heavenly kingdom, a beautiful existence that would be a reward for faithfulness. It is this latter viewpoint that was carried over into Christianity, and in a more materialistic sense, into modern science. The goal of historical change is some kind of utopian dream society in which evil will finally be overcome and perfect human bliss achieved. The Hebrew name for this outcome, arising out of the Mosaic Law and the Davidic kingdom, was the "Kingdom of God."

However, human sins and failings together with the universal history of humanity's continuing wars, invasions, and conquests, made that hope seem more and more remote. The prophetic dream was translated into some final intervention by the supreme divine being, whose original creation had somehow been disrupted. God would have no alternative left but to destroy evil men and nations, and institute a perfect society in which, as Isaiah pictured it[1]:

The wolf and the lamb will dwell together,
and the leopard rest among young goats; the calf and lion
cub will feed together,
and little children will take care of them.
The cow and the bear will be friendly,
and their young sleep peacefully together;
while the lion will graze on straw like cattle.

The infant will play near the cobra's hole,
and young children leap above
the viper's nest.
There shall be no hurt nor harm in Zion,
my holy mountain, says the Lord:
for the whole land will be filled with
the knowledge of the Lord,
as water fills the sea.

Jeremiah, who prophesied in the southern kingdom of Judah about a century after Isaiah, had the misfortune to be in public life as an interpreter of God's will and ways during the rise of the great Babylonian Empire and its domination of the Middle East. His writings, too, are full of dire warnings of impending doom for the nation and the people, but these are interspersed with words of encouragement and hope. He witnessed the first and second sieges of Jerusalem, and the carrying off into exile of all the more important officials and leading citizens, not only once but twice (597 and 587 B.C.E.) The fact that Jeremiah had counseled the king against rebellion is perhaps what led to his not being included among those deported. Later, however, a superpatriot, Ishmael, assassinated Gedaliah, whom the Babylonians had left in charge of their Judean province. But when this usurper, fearing Babylonian reprisals, fled with his supporters to Egypt, they took Jeremiah with them against his will. The last we hear of this notable prophet is found in forty-fourth chapter of his book, where he preaches against the Judean women who had returned to the idolatry of making sacrifices to Ishtar, the Egyptian "Queen of Heaven."

But before all that had happened, Jeremiah had some hopeful and encouraging things to say to the people whose lives and dreams had been so radically disrupted. He predicted a much better future for those who maintained their trust and commitment to their God. This is what he said:

Listen to the word of the Lord, you nations,
proclaim it to the distant coastlands.
He who scattered Israel will again bring them together
and watch over them as a shepherd guards his flock.

For the Lord has rescued Jacob
and saved him from an enemy stronger that he. .
They will come with great jubilation to Mount Zion,
radiant at the goodness of God:
the grain, wine and olive oil,
and the fertility of their flocks and herds.
They will be like a well-irrigated garden,
never being in want again.
Young maidens will dance for joy,
and young men and old will celebrate.
I shall comfort them by turning their grief into
gladness; and their mourning into happiness.
I shall satisfy their priests with rich food
and my people will have their fill of blessings.
This is the word of the Lord.[2]

While Jeremiah stayed behind in the stricken city and
preached both threats and promises to the people that were left,
one of the priests of Yahweh, who had been carried off along with
the treasure of the Temple and the gold of the palaces, together
with their inhabitants, was doing the same in the village of
Telabib situated on the banks of the river Chebar, a canal that carried water from the Euphrates to the city of Nippur, southeast of
Babylon. His writings reveal him as something of a mystic and
eccentric whose visions caused him to be carried in imagination
back to Jerusalem and then return again to Babylon. One of his
visions that is more remembered than most is that of being carried by the Spirit to a plain covered with the dry bones of people

who had been slain in the battles of Judah's destruction.[3] It is thus remembered because it became the basis for a well-known Afro-American spiritual, "Dry Bones." In the vision, as in the spiritual, the people and nation, which had been destroyed, would be restored. They would come back to life again.

Even more significantly, in the second part of the thirty-seventh chapter, the prophet describes a symbolic action he was instructed to carry out. He was to make a wooden tablet of two leaves, and on one leaf write: "Judah and the Israelites associated with him," and on the other leaf: "Joseph, the leaf of Ephraim and all the Israelite tribes." He was to join the two leaves together to form a folding tablet. When his fellow exiles would ask what he meant by this symbolic action he was to tell them that God had said:

I am taking the leaf of Joseph and the other tribes of Israel and joining it to the leaf of Judah and making them one tablet which shall be in my hand… I shall make them one nation in the land, on the mountains of Israel, and one king will be over them all… Thus they will be my people, and I shall be their God.

Then he continued:

I shall make an eternal treaty with them to guarantee their security and prosperity. I shall greatly increase their numbers and I shall put my temple in their midst forever.[4]

Such actions of the prophets, designed to bring encouragement to the people of the land with promises of an end to their troubles and better days ahead, gave rise to a new type of writing, borrowing from the prophetic techniques of visions and pronouncements, but carrying it further as times grew worse, suffering more intense and hope more dim. This is given the label: "eschatology," derived from *eschatos*, the Greek word for "last," and *logos*, Greek for "word," hence meaning "words about last things," or "knowledge of end times." The main biblical examples of this type of literature are the Old Testament book of Daniel, and the New Testament Revelation to John. There are a few other examples, such as Mark 13 and its parallels in Matthew and Luke, II Thessalonians 2, and II Peter 3 in the New Testament. Also included are chapters 12 through 14 of Zechariah plus Isaiah, chapters 24 through 27, in the Old Testament. Additionally there is much more literature of this type in the period between the Old and the New Testament writings, as well as following the New Testament time.

Another name for this kind of writing, because of its emphasis on the visionary experiences of the writers, is "Apocalypse," meaning revelation. This comes from the first word in the original Greek version of the last book of the Bible, "Apocolypsis."

Characteristic of this literature was to become more specific regarding what would happen and when it would happen as the life of the faithful became more intolerable. For example, the last book in our Christian Bible, which as we have noted gave a name to this type of thinking, arose during the administration of the Roman Emperor Domitian, 81-96 C.E.

Though earlier emperors from the time of Augustus (30 B.C.E. to 14.) onward had cultivated an "Emperor cult," and had been given honor as "gods" after their deaths, Domitian was the first who, during his lifetime, claimed for himself that he was divine, and a son of the Roman god, Jupiter. This did not trouble most of the inhabitants of the Roman Empire, who simply added the emperor to their pantheon of gods, but Domitian became quite provoked with those who refused to burn incense to his images, or render him homage as something more than a human being like themselves. This led him to expel people of the Jewish faith from Rome and since Christians were widely regarded as a sect of Judaism, the order included them. Even patricians of notable Roman families, such as the Flavians, came under suspicion because of their apparent sympathies with the Christians. Archaeological evidence has been uncovered that a Christian cemetery in Rome was the gift of Flavia Domitilla, wife of the Roman consul, Flavius Clemens. Though she was actually a niece of the emperor, she and her husband were both included in the order for exile.

Roman records restrict Domitian's orders for expulsion of Jews and others to the city of Rome, but it is evident that the cult of imperial divinity quickly spread to other provinces of the Empire, and was especially popular in Asia Minor, where a shrine in Domitian's honor was built in Ephesus, and games and festivals throughout the area honored him with acclamation and probably with liturgical rites as well.

Persecution and execution of Christians, among others, for their "godlessness," continued after the death of Domitian and on into the reign of succeeding emperors, as indicated by correspondence that has been preserved, which passed between the Emperor Trajan (98-117 C.E.) and his imperial legate, Pliny the Younger, in the provinces of Pontus and Bithynia, concerning how to deal with accused and/or convicted Christians. The best evidence is that it was somewhere during this decade, 90-100 C.E., that the Book of Revelation was written and published, as well as other New Testament books such as Hebrews and I Peter.

All of this literature was designed to encourage the believers in Christ as Lord who were thus threatened with official sanctions, and to help them to remain faithful to their respective churches. The Apocalypse or Revelation to John is an outstanding example of this fact. It begins with a series of letters to churches in Asia Minor. These were not, in all likelihood, copies of actual letters sent by John to these various churches, but rather examples of the kind of problems they faced in their own situations. That is the reason he selects seven of the churches to be addressed, not that they were the only ones in trouble, but as representative of all the churches. Seven was a number that had a special significance to the author in a mystical sense, as he uses it throughout the book: seven churches, seven seas, seven trumpets, seven bowls, seven visions of the dominion of the dragon, seven visions of the coming of the Son of Man, seven visions of the fall of "Babylon," and seven visions of the "end." Such symbolism, no doubt, veiled references to various historical events known to the reader, or various persons they knew, but the meaning becomes more obscure the farther the reader is removed from the actual events that were taking place. That is why the book has been subjected to such a variety of interpretations throughout the last two millennia, as those who have studied it have applied its symbolism to their own time. But the aim of the author was not so much to predict the future as to bring meaning to what was taking place in his own time. As the scholars Howard McKee and Franklin Young point out in their book, Understanding the New Testament: "The genius of ...the author of Revelation ...was not primarily foresight, but insight into the real nature of the problems confronting the Christian Community."[5] His aim was primarily to give hope to that community in the crisis situation they faced because of the power of the state, which was directed against them.

The symbolic language of this book, picturing a heavenly throne room, a lamb, a dragon, and a woman, the famous "four horsemen of the Apocalypse," scrolls and seals, beasts and "Babylon," judgment, and the "new Jerusalem," served two purposes. They had meaning to believers schooled in Christian teachings, but they were obscure enough not to give the emperor's agents sufficient evidence to charge believers with breaking Roman laws. However, they are also obscure enough that they give later Christians, brought up in a different climate of tolerance rather than persecution, opportunity to choose other meanings for them. This, we know, is what has happened to the interpretation of the Book of the Revelation to John through the last two millennia. It has provided enough fodder to produce the chaff of

The End of Time

outlandish interpretations that has misled thousands of New Testament readers and has given rise to numerous new sects and denominations in Christianity.

However wild such interpretations may be, and lacking in a foundation of the understanding of Christian history, they still give to the credulous an unshakable belief in the imminent end of the world as we know it, and, after many more disasters, natural and manmade, the return of the heavenly Son of Man in a cloud from heaven and the inauguration of the reign of God over the planet and all of life, human and otherwise, on it. Naturally, of course, those who proclaim these views expect to be numbered among the few thousand who will be saved from the fate of the rest and will enter into the rewards of the faithful in that new regime. But, many will say, the gospels make clear that Jesus, too, shared in this belief that the end of the old order was at hand and a "new age," was dawning in which the power of evil was to be overcome and the reign of God was to be triumphant throughout the earth. Ever since Albert Schweitzer published his scholarly study, The Quest of the Historical Jesus, early in the twentieth century, scholars have had to acknowledge that Jesus was an eschatologist and his teaching was colored by that fact.[6]

This conclusion, however, indicates that Jesus was human, which was affirmed at the beginning of Chapter 5, where we dealt with his biography. Therefore, he shared in the heritage of his people, and their thought categories, as we would expect. Yet he did not go to the extremes some of his later interpreters have done. He believed the new age of God's dominion was "at hand," as he said. But he declined to make any firm predictions as to when it would happen, as indicated in the quotation at the head of this chapter.

Like many other perceptive persons of his time, Jesus could see that the Roman domination of their Holy Land was becoming more and more galling to the Judeans, and would inevitably lead to conflict which the Romans with their legions could quickly bring to an end. After all there had been a rebellion in Galilee, which ended in the destruction of Sepphoris, only a few miles from Nazareth where Jesus was growing up. Though perhaps only from ten to twelve years old at the time, he could not forget the rebels hanging on crosses along the roads leading out of that city. Much of the content of predictions that probably can be attributed to Jesus in the Gospels dealt with the coming destruction of Jerusalem which he could foresee and which came to pass in 70 AD, some forty years after his own death on a cross. He believed that God would intervene to save his people, but he probably did not foresee that this salvation would come in the form of the rapid growth of a community of his own followers, and converts to his teaching, that would embrace not only his own fellow Jews, but even the much-hated Romans, and their Greek subjects. It is we, looking back to that history from our own time, who may well recognize the hand of God in creative relationships which brought about the potential for the still unrealized dominion of Creative Relationship in our world.

Still, we may ask, is there any scientific basis for this eschatology, or doctrine of last things, which underlies so much of the New Testament, and parts of the Old Testament as well? The answer to that question goes back to the work of Clausius, Helmholtz, and Kelvin, whose studies in the mid-19th century on thermodynamics, and the development of the Second Law of Thermodynamics, the degradation of energy into heat, which is dissipated, led to the concept of the heat-death of the universe. This was called the increase of entropy by Clausius.[7]

This settled for all time the question of whether the universe was cyclical or progressive and introduced the concept of the "arrow of time" into present-day cosmology and physics. The arrow of time means that space/time, the physicist's concept of the universe, goes in one direction only. It might possibly, in quantum dynamics, reverse direction if the universe should ever stop expanding and begin to contract instead. In that case entropy might well decrease instead of increase.

As a matter of fact, however, another scientist, a biologist this time, by the name of Charles Darwin, was, at just that period of human history, bringing forth a concept that evolution was counteracting the degradation of energy by building simple forms of life into more complex ones. As this point of view caught on, chemists, physicists, astronomers, and cosmologists, began to see that there was evolution in their fields of science as well. The dissipation of energy into heat that is lost forever in warming up the universe slightly can be and is counteracted in directing that energy into more creative directions. And that is what Creative Relationship, which we have identified as God, is doing in the universe.

It is not, however, certain that humanity will inherit the fruits of that creativity into the indefinite future. Many species, from trilobites to dinosaurs, have come and gone before, and many are disappearing even now because of the destructive nature of many of our human activities. Unless human beings, who have been given more freedom to choose their course than any other earthly beings before them, do better than they have been doing in cooperating in the work of God (Creative Relationship), their time on Earth, which has been very short in the lifetime of the universe, and much less than that of other species that have come and gone, may soon come to a bitter end.

But, even if we should become wise enough to reduce our numbers and husband the resources of our spaceship Earth, the earth itself will not last forever. Cosmologists, studying the birth and death of stars, have come to the conclusion that our Sun, at about four and a half billion years of age, has already used up about half of its projected lifetime. As it uses up its hydrogen fuel, transforming it into helium, it will eventually burn out. The process it will go through, they predict, will be to expand into a cooler, but still very hot red ball that will engulf its nearer planets, including Earth, and burn them to a crisp. Then it will blow off its outer layers and shrink into a white dwarf star, surrounded by its children of nine or ten dead planets. Unless space-traveling humans have found their way to an earthlike planet of some other, and younger, star before that, it may well be the end of human history. But, even if they do find a home in some other corner of the universe, that universe itself will ultimately come to an end, perhaps by expanding until all galaxies are separated by more than twenty billion lightyears, and die out, or, maybe, by turning the corner of outward travel and coming back to a final huge singularity, in about the time it took it to expand. Such a span of time is virtually inconceivable to individuals like ourselves who have spans of life one hundred billionth as long.

Only if we become one with God (Creative Relationship) who has, possibly, created other universes, and will continue to do so, as in the one we are just beginning to know and understand well, will our existence be eternal and become perfect.

––––––––

[1] Isaiah 11:6-9.

[2] Jeremiah 31:10-14.

[3] Ezekiel 37:1-14.

[4] Ibid., vss. 19, 22, 23b, 26.

[5] H. C. Kee and F. W. Young, (1957) Understanding the New Testament, Englewood Cliffs, NJ p. 454. Prentice Hall, Inc.

[6] Scweitzer, Albert, (1910) The Quest of the Historical Jesus, A.& G. Black).

[7] Rudolf Clausius, Herman Helmholz, and William Thompson (Lord Kelvin) were physicists, two German and one Scottish, who between 1847 and 1852 developed the principle of the conservation of energy from the work of Carnot and Joule in studying thermodynamics.

CHAPTER TEN

WHERE DO WE GO FROM HERE?

"If the Word was made flesh, then all flesh may be made the instruments of the Word." –Lynn Harold Hough

Those of you who have followed the course of this book from the beginning have seen how a Divine Master Plan, which we have called Creative Relationship, has been in effective operation since the very first milliseconds of the Big Bang to bring about the complexity of the Universe as we know it. Energy coalesced into little packets that we now know as *quanta*. These little bundles of energy gave rise to protons, neutrons, and electrons as well as their antimatter counterparts. But in the economy of the Creator, matter, in the form of atoms and chemical molecules, predominated as the explosive universe cooled. As it cooled even further these scattered molecular particles were drawn together by gravity to form immense clouds. As these particles were drawn together into more closely packed masses they interacted by atomic fusion to form nuclear furnaces called stars where further, more complex, atoms could be made. When some of these incandescent aggregations of matter became too large and quickly burned up their atomic fuel, they exploded into novas and supernovas, blasting their chemicals into space where they could soon gather together to form smaller suns and planets in orbit around them. These are solar systems, which are the cradles of the self-replicating molecules called life.

Our planet Earth turned out to be one of these. Scientists, in the last century and a half on earth, have discovered how these complex living chemicals formed the immense variety of microbes, plants, and animals which have colonized our planet from its icy polar regions to its tropics. They have also seen how there evolved new and more specialized forms that could eventually develop the brains and self-consciousness to become the scientists who could begin to unravel life's mysteries.

We, the species of the primate family, who are the products of this development, first learned how to walk with an upright stance, and then to use our forelimbs to manipulate objects, some of which could be fashioned into tools. Early humans also learned the art of communication, formulating sounds into words and words into sentences with which they could first talk to one another, and then, through the formation of symbols that stood for sounds, to write messages that could be understood by their family members and larger groups called tribes.

Thus began a new kind of cultural evolution, which speeds up the process of adaptation to new environmental challenges by relying on the survival, in human communication, of certain cultural units, dubbed memes by the noted zoologist, Richard Dawkins.[1] A meme, which has a similarity in sound to gene, is a remembered concept, which becomes a node or pattern in the neuron linkage of the human brain and is communicated by language to other humans to be handed down from generation to generation. Not only intellectual concepts, but also socially acceptable patterns of behavior can be passed on in this way. They then become the medium of a cultural heritage.

This process took a long, long time, for progress was slow in the protohuman species such as homo habilis, homo erectus, homo ergaster, and homo neanderthalensis. It began to speed up gradually as our own species, homo sapiens, came on the scene. Our cultural evolution began very slowly with only small steps such as fashioning stone tools and weapons, and learning to control and use fire. These primitive advances were followed only after long intervals of little or no progress by improvements in the fashioning of stone tools and developing improved weapons and hunting techniques. The first technological industry for the fashioning of stone tools apparently arose among the homo erectus subspecies some 700,000 years ago, though a sporadic use of stone tools is indicated among their predecessors, *homo habilis*, in Africa perhaps more than a million years ago. Marked improvements in the fashioning of stone implements apparently took tens of thousands, or even hundreds of thousands of years to make.

The *paleolithic* or "Old Stone Age" began approximately 2.4 million years ago in Africa where the earliest hominid, homo habilis, used sharpened stone flakes to cut the meat of scavenged animals, and left their tools to be found by anthropologists more than two thousand millennia later.

In about a half million years their bigger and smarter successors, called *homo erectus* by the anthropologists, had developed larger stones, sharpened on one end, as hand axes and hammers. Their increased skill in the use of tools, and their greater cleverness also made them more successful hunters. They spread out from Africa to Europe and southeast Asia, where they used fire to drive herds of animals and, after a successful hunt, to roast the meat.

There were minor refinements in stone toolmaking, but no startling advances for the next million years, then a new technique was developed among the predecessors of *homo sapiens* in Africa and spread among that species wherever they had settled. *Homo neanderthalensis*, appearing first in Africa, then in Europe about 120,000 years ago, developed toolkits of relatively high quality and variety, but the major advance took place when *homo sapiens sapiens* appeared on the European scene around 40,000 years ago. These early representatives of modern man also developed a startling advance in art by painting lifelike figures of animals on the walls of hidden recesses in their cave dwellings.

It appears likely that some systematic exploration of natural laws also began to take place among these earliest modern humans of 40,000 years ago, who had developed their communication skills to a higher level, but the really rapid scientific advance awaited the arrival of the Greek and Hellenic cultures of about 2600 years ago. Its advance was sporadic, however, until the time of Galileo in Renaissance Italy in the early seventeenth century. A tangible symbol of this advance was Galileo's use of an improved telescope to see Earth's moon close up as well as the satellites of Saturn and Jupiter and the phases of Venus. A charter was given to the Royal Society of London in 1662 to formalize the curiosity of the experimental early scientists and led to a population boom among the European nations by the beginning of the eighteenth century. The discovery of the circulation of the blood in 1628, the microscope in 1660, and the gravitational theory of Newton in 1682 began to bring major advances in science. Experiments in regulating air pressure and making vacuums at about the beginning of the eighteenth century, plus the discovery of oxygen in 1771 led to a rapid rise in technology. All this heralded the rapid breakthroughs in science and technology that have marked the nineteenth and twentieth centuries.

No individual who has lived through a large portion of the twentieth century can ignore the rapid advances in technology that have taken place during this period. For example, when I studied geology at the University of Wisconsin in the 1930's, Alfred Wegener's theory of "continental drift" brought forth amused smiles if not outright laughter. Now, of course, he has been vindicated and the study of plate tectonics is a major part of the geologist's discipline.

At the beginning of the century in 1901, telephones and

automobiles were rare. Airplanes came into being at Kitty Hawk, North Carolina, in 1903. In 1905 a humble patent clerk in Switzerland named Albert Einstein proved that light consisted of tiny particles (or quanta) called photons. He also replaced Newton's theory of gravity with an outlandish theory of curved space-time and called it relativity. Matter, he said, was but a solid form of energy, and the equation expressing this mathematically was $E = mc^2$, meaning that energy equals the mass times the square of the speed of light in a vacuum. Electronics dawned a year later with the invention of the triode vacuum tube. Radio, and then television, exploded upon the world, together with a new means of calculating and writing information called the computer. The structure of the genes, the basis of reproduction and of evolution in all life, was discovered in 1953, which was the same year of the invention of the H-bomb capable of wiping life from Earth. Combining such weapons with the much older science of rocketry led to the threat of global nuclear warfare, which still is a problem for international relationships. But rockets were also made capable of carrying humans outside the environs of Earth, landing men on the Moon, and research vehicles on Mars. Together with the discovery of the causes of many diseases, and the means of their eradication, the twentieth century has proven to be a period of great advance in science and technology. Without doubt this progress is only a herald of the triumphs of human ingenuity in the twenty-first century if only humans can bring about the more constructive relationships between people which will help us to use them wisely.

As we stand on the threshold of a new century—and a new millenium—the question before us is "Where do we go from here?" What should be our aim and objective as the dominant species of life on planet Earth for whatever future we may have left?

Surely our overall goal must be to further advance that Creative Relationship which produced our universe and brought us to our present place in it. In the Christian religious terminology, which is part of most of the western culture in which I, and many of you who are the readers of these words, were brought up, it is to advance the Kingdom of God. We have made remarkable progress in our scientific knowledge and technological expertise. We have not done anywhere near as well in the advancement of human relationships. Crime and cruelty, hatred and violence, jealousy and strife still mark many of our relationships with other humans, especially if they have some cultural or religious differences from us. Sadly, even religions which were formed to bring us together in furthering some over-riding noble objective have turned out to be a cause for our divisions and lack of understanding in dealing with each other.

It might be well, then, to call for a moratorium on some of our scientific and technological goals, such as interplanetary travel for example, until we have developed the moral and ethical expertise we might need to deal with advanced forms of life in other parts of the universe. First we have to develop the cultural capacity to get along with other humans on this planet!

To bring about such a radical change in our human nature and its cultural expression we have to find some universal goal toward which all races, classes, and religious organizations can strive. What better one could there be than the great spiritual reality, which brought about the creation of the universe and our presence in it as an end product of the great evolutionary stream of life. We, alone in the universe so far as we know, are the sentient, thoughtful, forward-looking and planning beings, which could conceive and hopefully achieve such a goal. If we can do it, and we have to do it together if it is to be done, we will begin to live up to the scientific label which we have put upon our own species, *homo sapiens sapiens*, which means "wise, wise humans."

Before that can happen, however, we will have to address our mental and ethical inheritance to a few intractable problems.

One of the most pressing of these is that of the overcrowding of our planet by our species and the consequent destruction of its environment that is essential to all life. Unfortunately many of our religious and political leaders have a tendency to minimize this problem and to say lightly, "We have always managed to adjust to change before. We can do so again." To do that is to ignore the facts as our science has ascertained them.

Back at the beginning of the seventeenth century, when science was in its infancy, the estimated world population was about 500,000. It had expanded geometrically to 1.7 billion three hundred years later at the beginning of the twentieth century. By 1970 it had ballooned to more than twice that figure, 3.65 billion. At the end of the twentieth century it is more than six billion!

When you are flying in an airplane across the country and leave behind the metropolitan area, you are struck, nevertheless, by the space that still is vacant down below.

It seems that there is plenty of room for more people. Ecologists, however, use a formula, PAT, for measuring the impact of more people on the environment. This formula represents population numbers *times* the affluence per capita (their rate of consumption) *times* a measure of how much technology they use in attaining that level of consumption. This gives the expert a way of determining the "ecological footprint" of a given population in supporting each of its members in their standard of living, or the standard they would like to attain. In the comparatively wealthy United States this means that the average person requires five hectares of area (12.355 acres) to sustain his or her lifestyle. In most of the poorer countries of Africa or Asia that "footprint" is about 1.25 acres. Of course those are developing countries, which means they would like to bring their standard up to the American level. With the present world population, to raise all of the people to the present U.S. level would take two more planets with the size and resources of Earth!

The problem is that the *present* population of the earth is rapidly exhausting its resources of minerals, fossil fuels, potable water, and breathable air. We are also polluting much of the land with our refuse, including nuclear waste, so that it is no longer useful in sustaining us. And we have no other planet Earth to move to when ours is no longer livable.

This, then, is the critical problem for our existence into the twenty-first century and beyond. For the environmental experts among us who can clearly see the hand-writing on the wall, the myopia of most of our political and religious leaders who ignore it is very troubling. They may wait to do anything about it until it is too late.

Solving the complex problems involved in reversing the present trends is a goal that will require the concentrated attention of the best minds of our day, scientific, philosophical, sociological, theological, and mathematical.

One difficulty is that having many children is instinctive biological behavior. Men and women sought to have large families because that insured the survival of their genes generation after generation. Even now the reason so many couples in the more destitute parts of the world have so many children is because these are their means of insuring their social security. When they get too old to work and grow crops, herd animals or hunt them, their sons and daughters will take care of them, they think. It may not always happen that way, but the more children they have the more likely it is to happen in the way they anticipate and hope. But to let that kind of thinking go on indefinitely will only lead to the overcrowding of the earth and less of its limited resources to be distributed among its inhabitants.

What can be done to solve this problem? Unless we all want to follow the example of the post World War II Chinese Communist government and install a dictatorship that will enforce each family to have no more than one child, mandating abortions for those who step out of line to conceive more children, we will have to establish, to the satisfaction of all our people, that too many children are an ecological hazard. A rate of no more than two offspring per family will stabilize the population at its present level. Some, however, will not be able to have any children of their own, and some children will not have children in their turn for one reason or another. This will mean a gradual reduction in the number of people worldwide and that is the most desirable outcome. If such a course is followed in the twenty-first century, the world population may well be lowered to about 2.6 billion by that century's end. That is about what the world population was in 1950, and is a much more reasonable figure than what we have now, and much less of a disaster than what we would have if present trends continue unabated. With the expected worldwide growth in technology and energy usage, even a further reduction in human population would be advisable for the rest of the third millenium for humanity to survive as a living species and to realize its full potential.

Besides solving the difficult problem of reducing our numbers, what else should we be doing to further creative relationships throughout our world? Though each of us must do our own part in reducing population numbers by choosing to have smaller families, the motivating of this conservative action on a worldwide scale will take the commitment and wisdom of the world's political and religious leaders. Individually we cannot do much about it. However, there remains much left to be done by each one of us.

With ever more persistence and urgency we will have to continue to do what we have begun to do in finding alternative sources of energy, which will help to save our natural resources for future generations, prevent the pollution of our atmosphere and waters, make more and better use of the arable land to grow food without depleting the soil or rendering it infertile, protect the habitat of other species as well as our own, because we depend on them as much as they do on us, and to distribute the wealth more equitably between the various races, classes, and nations. In short, we have to dedicate ourselves, individually, to discovering and bringing to pass more creative relationships between one another and the world around us. Yet, even before that, we will have to strive mightily to rid ourselves and our children, who will shape the future, of all those destructive relationships that have for so long impeded the work of God (Creative Relationship) in our world.

In our wealth of human literature, including our Bible and the sacred literature of other cultures and ethnic groups, such as the Koran, the Upanishads, the Buddhist and Confucian teachings, along with many others, we can find numerous examples of constructive living, as well as those of the destructive kind. We can also look to the great humanitarians of history for models to be emulated in our own lives. For example, not long before these words were written, humans around the world were shocked and saddened by the deaths of two such persons who, under very different circumstances, lived in a creative, constructive way by helping people less fortunate than themselves. One was an aristocrat of English descent, Princess Diana, whose life was cut short in a tragic accident. The other was Mother Theresa, a Roman Catholic nun who organized charitable ministries among the destitute people of India. Each, in her own fashion, exhibited a deep concern for the poor and suffering, not just in a theoretical way, but by going among them to relieve their pain. "Yes," some would say, "but those two persons were living in unusual circumstances which gave them special opportunities for their humanitarian work." This is not strictly true, however. What happened in those two instances were not special opportunities for service, but rather unusual circumstances for public notice; each of them received a large amount of publicity. Others have probably done as much or more without such widespread recognition of their work.

We, too, will often find opportunities in everyday life where we can provide either material help to those in need, or at least some means of giving them hope and encouragement. All that we need do is to watch out for those opportunities and respond to them. Jesus, in telling his parable about the final judgment (Matt. 25:31-40) said: "I was hungry and you gave me food, I was thirsty and you gave me something to drink, I was a stranger and you welcomed me into your home. I was sick and you took care of me. I was in prison and you visited me." Then the righteous asked, "When did all this take place?" He responded, "Whenever you did these things for one of the least important among you, you did them for me." Helping a neighbor who is sick or in trouble, even if we don't like that person very much, will qualify as building creative relationships, whether on not we receive public notice or praise for the deed.

Furthermore such opportunities will come to us in our place of business, in a store where we work or shop, in community activities or recreational ones, as well as in our neighborhoods. Especially in our homes and in our daily family life, where we spend most of our time, they are to be found every day.

Earlier chapters in this book have given us clues as to what kind of individual conduct is needed to make a creative contribution as to what God as Creative Relationship is doing in our present-day world. The Bible, too, gives us many specific examples of what can be accomplished for a better society and a more peaceful, harmonious world, not only by national and religious leaders but by ordinary human beings in normal circumstances. All that we need to do is to exercise our imaginations and bend our energies to accomplishing the good and helpful deeds that we can easily find to do in our normal, everyday life. Thus we can and will become partners with God in His/Her creative work. In the words of great philosophers and religious teachers who have guided human behavior for more than twenty millennia, we only have to enhance our virtues and eliminate our sins. This, rather than the accumulation of wealth and power, which is the primary goal of so many among us, will have to become our dominant passion if humanity is to realize its God-given potential.

NOT THE END, WE HOPE

---

[1] Richard Dawkins, (1986) The Blind Watchmaker, New York. p. 158.

Bibliography

Asimov, Isaac. (1984). *Asimov's New Guide to Science*, (revised edition). New York: Basic Books.

Asimov, Isaac. (1965). *The Human Brain*. New York: Mentor Books.

Auel, Jean. (1981). *The Clan of the Cave Bear*. New York: Bantam Books.

Auel, Jean. (1982).*The Valley of Horses*. New York: Crown Publishers Inc.

Beiser, Arthur. (1986). *The Earth*. (revised edition), New York: Life Nature Library, Time-Life Books.

Bergamini, David. (1967). *The Universe*.(revised edition), New York: Life Nature Library, Time-Life Books.

Bornkamm, Gunther. (1960). *Jesus of Nazareth*. New York: Harper & Brothers.

Breuer, Reinhard. (1991). *The Anthropic Principle*. Cambridge, MA: Birkhauser Boston, Inc.
    [Originally published in German in Munich (1981) by Myster Verflag Gmbh.]

Bronkowski, Jacob. (1973). *The Ascent of Man*. Boston: Little, Brown and Company.

Bultmann, Rudolf Karl. (1960). *Jersus Christ and Mythology*. London:

Calder, Nigel. (1984). *Timescale*. New York: Simon and Schuster

Campbell, Jeremy, (1982). *Grammatical Man*. New York: Simon and Schuster.

Cambpbell, Joseph. (1988) *The Power of Myth*. (with Bill Moyer). New Yorl:

Chaisson, Eric. (1981) *Cosmic Dawn*. Boston/Toronto: Little, Brown and Company.

Clark, William Newton. (1925) *An Outline of Christian Theology*. New York: Scribner's.

Darwin, Charles. (1979) *The Illustrated Origin of Species*.(abridged and introduced by Richard E.Leakey). New York: Hill and Wang.

Davies, Paul. (1981) *The Edge of Infinity*. New York: Simon and Schuster

Davies, Paul. (1984) *Superforce.* New York: Simon and Schuster

Dawkins, Richard. (1986) *The Blind Watchmaker.* New York, London: W.W. Norton & Company

Dow, Robert Arthur. (1971) *Learning Through Encounter.* Valley Forge, PA: Judson Press.

Einstein, Albert. (1979) *A Centenary Volume.* Cambridge, MA: Harvard University Press.

Emiliani, Cesare. (1992) *Planet Earth.* Cambridge, U.K. and New York: Press Syndicate of the University of Cambridge.

Enslin, Morton Scott. (1938) *Christian Beginnings.* New York: Harper and Brothers.

Farb, Peter. (1967) *Ecology.* (revised edition), New York: Life Nature Library, Time-Life Books.

Garnett, A. Campbell. (1942) *A Realistic Philosophy of Religion.* Chicago: Willet, Clark.

Garnett, A. Campbell. (1945) *God In Us.* Chicago: Willett, Clark

Gribbin, John. (1983) *Spacewarps.* New York: Delacorte Press/Eleanor Friede

Howell, F. Clark. (1968). *Early Man.* (revised edition), New York: Life Nature Library, Time-Life Books.

Moore, Ruth. (1968). *Evolution.* (revised edition), New York: Life Nature Library, Time-Life Books.

Hunt, Morton. (1982) *The Universe Within.* New York: Simon and Schulster.

Jacobsen, Thorkild. (1945) "Mesopotamiam Religion", *An Enclyclopidia of Religion,* edited by Vergilius Ferm. New York: The Philosophical Library.

Kaufmann, William J., III. (1979) *Black Holes and Warped Spacetime.* San Francisco: W.H. Freeman.

Kee, H.C. and F.W. Young. (1957) *Understanding the New Testament.* Englewood Cliffs, NJ: Prentice Hall, Inc.

Kerwin, Carlotta, editor. (1972) *The Emergence of Man Series*: "Life Before Man", vol 1. "The Missing Link," vol.2. "The First Men,"vol.3. "The Neanderthals," vol. 4. "Cro-Magnon Man," vol. 5.

Knowles, Malcolm and Hulda, (1959) *Introduction to Group Dynamics.* New York: Association Press.

Kohler, Wolfgang. (1947) *Gestalt Psychology.* New York: Mentor Books

Krupp, Edwin. (1983) *Echoes of Ancient Skies.* "THe Gods We Worship," Chapter 3, New York: Harper and Row.

Meninger, Karl. (1983) *Whatever Became of Sin?* New York: Hawthorne Books, Inc.

Pelligrino, Charles (1985) *Time Gate.* Blue Ridge Summit, PA: TAB Books, Inc.

Pfeiffer, John. (1982) *The Creative Explosion.* New York: Harper and Row.

Planck, Max. (1962) *The Great Ideas of Today,* "The Universe in the Light of Modern Physics," Chicago: Encyclopedia Brittanica.

Resak, Richard. (1980) *The Brain: the Last Frontier.* New York: Warner Books.

Sagan, Carl. (1980) *Cosmos.* New York: Random House.

Sagan, Carl. (1977) *The Dragon of Eden.* New York: Rando, House.

Schweitzer, Albert. (1910) *The Quest of the Historical Jesus.* London: A. and C. Black.

Science and Creationism (1984) edited by Ashley Montagu. New York: Oxford University Press.

Sheehan, Thomas. (1986) *The First Coming.* New York: Dorsett Press.

Shipman, Harry. (1980) *Black Holes, Quasars, and the Universe,* second edition, Boston: Houghton Mifflin.

Smith, Anthony. (1984) *The Mind.* New York: Viking Press.

Trattner, Ernest. (1938) *The Story of the World's Great Thinkers.* New York: The Great Home Library

Trefil, James. (1980) *From Atoms to Quarks.* New York: Charles Scribner's Sons.

Wilson, Edward O. (1998) *Consilience: the unity of knowledge.* New York: Alfred A. Knopf, Inc.

Additional Suggested Reading

Atkins, Peter. (1992) *Creation Revisted.* New York/Oxford: W.H.

Coveney, Peter and Roger Highfield. (1990)*The Arrow of Time.* New York: Fawcett Columbine.

Davies, Paul. (1988) *The Cosmic Blueprint.* New York: Simon and Schulster.

Davies, Paul. (1992) *The Mind of God.* New York: Simon and Schuster.

Dennett, Daniel. (1995) *Darwin's Dangerous Idea.* New York: Simon and Schuster.

Diamon, Jared. (1992) *The Third Chimpanzee.* New York: HarperCollins.

Dyson, Freeman. (1988) *Infinite in All Directions.* New York: Harper and Row

Einstein, Albert. (1961) *Relativity.* New York: Crown Publishers, Inc.

Hawking, Stephen. (1988) *A Brief History of Time.* New York: Bantam Books

Herbert, Nick. (1985) *Quantum Reality*. Garden City, NY: Anchor Press/Doubleday.

Kafatos, Menas and Robert Nadeau. (1990) *The Conscious Universe*. New York: Springer-Verlag.

Kauffamn, Stuart. (1995) *At Home in The Universe*. New York: Oxford University Press.

Leslie, John. (1996) *The End of The World*. London/New York: Routledge.

Scott, Alwyn. (1995) *Stairway to the Mind*. New York: Springer-Verlag

Stanley, Steven. (1981) *The New Evolutionary Time Table*. New York: Basic Books.

Tipler, Frank. (1994) *The Physics of Immortality*. New York: Doubleday.